SUCCESSFUL TEAMWORK

HOW TO BECOME A TEAM PLAYER

SUCCESSFUL TEAMWORK

HOW TO BECOME A TEAM PLAYER

by Erik Chesla

LearningExpress

NEW YORK

Chesla, Erik.
    Successful Teamwork / by Erik Chesla.
    p.   cm. –
    ISBN 1-57685-204-0
Teams in the workplace. 2. Interpersonal relations.
3. Interpersonal communication.   4. Group problem solving.
5. Cooperation.   6. Employee empowerment.   I. Title.   II. Series.
HD66.C458   1999
650.1'3—dc21   99-11367
                                    CIP

Printed in the United States of America
9 8 7 6 5 4 3 2 1
First Edition

For Further Information
For information on LearningExpress, other LearningExpress products, or bulk sales, please write to us at:
    LearningExpress™
    900 Broadway
    Suite 604
    New York, NY 10003

Please visit LearningExpress on the World Wide Web at www.LearnX.com

ISBN 1-57685-204-0

CONTENTS

Introduction 1

Part I. An Introduction to Working with Others. 3

Chapter 1. The Collaborative Work Environment. 5

Chapter 2. The Benefits and Challenges of Working in Teams. 13

Part II. Communicating Effectively with Others 21

Chapter 3. The Communication Process 23

Chapter 4. Different of Points of View 31

Chapter 5. Saying What You Mean. 41

Chapter 6. Delivering Positive Messages with Power 51

Chapter 7. Tips for Conveying Bad or Negative News 59

Chapter 8. Tips for Effective Reports, Reviews, and Instructions 69

Chapter 9. Building Better Listening Skills 79

Chapter 10. Participating Successfully in Meetings 87

Chapter 11. Overcoming Common Barriers to Verbal
Communications. 99

Chapter 12. Overcoming Common Non-Verbal
Communication Barriers. 107

Part III. Working Effectively in Teams 115

Chapter 13. Stages of Team Development and Team Norms. . 117

Chapter 14. Team Member Roles 127

Chapter 15. Leadership and Teams. 137

Chapter 16. Communicating Effectively in Teams 147

Chapter 17. Resolving Team Conflict 157

Chapter 18. Effective Team Problem Solving 167

Chapter 19. Alternative Methods for Problem Solving
in Work Groups 175

Chapter 20. Evaluating and Improving Team Performance . . . 185

ADDITIONAL RESOURCES. 195

INTRODUCTION

Whether you run your own company, manage a department, or work as an administrative assistant, one thing is for sure: If you haven't worked as part of a team yet, you will very soon.

Most businesses, from Fortune 500 companies to local florists and every size and type of company in-between, rely on their employees' ability to work effectively with others in order to compete in an increasingly competitive marketplace.

Yet, while teamwork has become a building block for success in organizations everywhere, most employees have never had any formal teamwork training. Although many high school and college students work in study groups, in pairs with a lab partner, or even in formal project teams, they are usually not taught how to work effectively in a team.

If you have ever interacted with another person to schedule a meeting, or coordinated a get-together with several colleagues, then you know what it takes to interact with others in order to achieve a specific goal. In essence, that is what teamwork is all about: communicating, interacting, and working effectively with others to accomplish a shared goal.

Even if you consider yourself a pro when it comes to communicating with others and working in teams, then you know that continuous improvement is the key to future success. So whether you are very experienced at working productively in a team or are scared to death of participating in any group, you will find that this book will help you perform better at work, at home, and even at play. As a matter of fact, if you have to communicate, coordinate, and interact with anyone else to accomplish anything, you will find the readings, exercises, and examples in this book very helpful.

This book will give you the tools you need to:

- communicate more effectively with others at work
- be more productive in meetings
- improve your decision-making and problem-solving skills
- participate successfully in a team
- continue building your team skills for a lifetime of learning

Like other books in the Basics Made Easy series from LearningExpress, this book is most effective when used daily for a month. If you read one chapter and carefully complete the exercises for that chapter every day of the week (Monday through Friday), and use the weekends to review the material, you will find that your ability to work with others will increase tremendously, even in as short a time as a month.

PART I

AN INTRODUCTION TO WORKING WITH OTHERS

In this, the first section of the book, you will be introduced to a phenomenon in business evolution called empowerment. Companies of all sizes are empowering their employees—giving them access to as much information as possible and making sure they have the freedom, power, and tools to communicate openly with other employees, key vendors, and suppliers in order to make informed decisions and to continuously improve their organization. Companies are relying on the positive effects of teamwork and collaboration to get ahead of their competitors.

Along with empowerment and teamwork comes added responsibility—to communicate and motivate others you depend on to get your job done. You will also need to rely on strong critical-thinking and problem-solving skills in order to succeed in this empowered workplace.

Part I should give you a good *heads up* as to what skills you will need to survive the Information Revolution. It will also begin to get you thinking about the benefits and challenges of teamwork.

CHAPTER | 1

THE COLLABORATIVE WORK ENVIRONMENT

LEARNING OBJECTIVES

After reading this chapter you should be able to:

- understand how the Information Revolution has changed the way businesses work
- identify the differences between traditional organizations and *Learning Organizations*
- identify the new roles and responsibilities of employees in today's business environment

THE INFORMATION REVOLUTION

As the 21st century approaches, organizations of all sizes are changing the way they do business. With rapid advances in computer and communications technologies, organizations can now conduct business virtually anywhere in the world. They can utilize new technologies such as the Internet, videoconferencing, and even teleconferencing to work with virtual teams—groups of people who can work on the same project but may never be physically together at any point in the project. Take for example, the company that sold you your sneakers at the local mall. They may have headquarters in California, a production facility in Hong Kong, an advertising agency with members in England, Paris, New York, and Los Angeles, and Research & Development staff in Sao Paolo. Yet employees at all of these locations worked together to provide you with your sneakers.

Another effect of the Information Revolution is the ability for individuals, as citizens, employees, or consumers, to make informed decisions instantly. For example, in the past if you wanted to find out about your retirement account you had to fill out a request form and wait for days, or even weeks to get a response. If you wanted to make a change in your policy—forget about anything within a time period of less than a month. Now however, you can go online, from your home, virtually 24 hours a day and access real-time information. And if you want to make a change to your policy, today it takes only as long as clicking your mouse.

What does this mean for most organizations?

They have to change how they do business in order to continue to succeed. And in today's rapidly changing business environment, many organizations are empowering their employees by providing them with the information, tools, and training they need to make important business decisions on their own. In order to succeed, these organizations rely on teamwork and collaboration among their employees more than ever before.

What does this mean for you?

You have to change the way you work in order to be effective. Specifically, you have to know how to communicate effectively with others and work in a team environment. You will also need to be prepared to make important business (and personal) decisions and solve complicated problems by coordinating efforts outside of your immediate area of expertise.

THE LEARNING ORGANIZATION—EMPOWERING EMPLOYEES

Smart companies everywhere are empowering their employees at all levels, giving them more responsibility and teaching them how to work effectively in teams. These companies can be called *learning organizations*. By giving employees all the information they need to participate more fully in the day-to-day decisions of the company, these companies are allowing their employees to control their own destiny. They reward success by giving their employees more freedom and more power to make important business decisions. They invite, encourage, and reward continuous learning, and much of it is focused on so-called *soft skills*, such as leadership, effective communications, working with others, and problem solving.

In the past, power, information, and decision-making were reserved for executives and a few top managers in the company. The power to influence long-term strategic decisions as well as the power to influence day-to-day operational decisions rested mostly in the minority of top managers and executives. These veterans would protect and control their power over their subordinates. They virtually controlled the flow of information to colleagues and subordinates—carefully guarding who could have access to important data. Meanwhile, the majority of the employees—those directly working to produce and deliver the products and services that keep the company in business—had little or no power to make decisions.

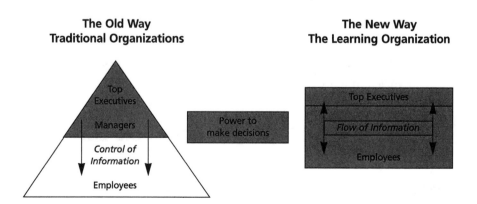

Practice:

1. Can you think of examples where sharing information, instead of guarding it, helps get things done better, faster, or for less money?

2. In comparison to the traditional organization, where employees were only given the basic information they needed to perform specific tasks, how are employees' jobs different if they have access to corporate-wide information and are expected to make important decisions on their own?

Answers:

1. If you are a customer service representative for virtually any company that supplies goods or services to consumers, you could certainly help a customer with a problem much more effectively if you had all their account information available on your PC the second that the call comes through. It would also help if you could access information about your products or services via your PC rather than having to call a supervisor or look up answers in any other format.

2. Having access to more information and being expected to make important business decisions assumes that you have the necessary skills to make sense of the data and use the information wisely before making an informed decision. Communication skills become much more important in this situation. Employees' jobs are also different under this scenario because they have much more responsibility. Their actions and input effect more than just their own job area so their skills and knowledge base has to be broader—because they are involved in more than just their own tasks.

Example of a learning organization: the Cissa Corporation

If the Cissa Corporation were a traditional company that has many levels of managers and does not empower their employees to make key decisions, Charlie Parks, the shift manager at the assembly line, certainly wouldn't be able to authorize a purchase of a new air conditioner for the shop floor when the old one breaks. He would have to fill out the proper forms and pass the request up the chain of command, where it would eventually end up with Phil Omman, the vice president of operations, who would then make a decision. Days, even weeks would pass until the problem would be addressed.

However, since Cissa is a learning organization, and workers are empowered to make their own decisions, the same problem would be treated much differently. Charlie would have more information available to him and he would have more power to deal with the problem directly (with the help of his work team). In this case, Charlie would be a member of the Operations Empowerment Team, where he would meet with Phil and other executives to share information and make recommendations about the operations of the company. Charlie would also be the facilitator of the Line Empowerment Team, a team of shift workers focused on improving the working conditions on the assembly line at the plant.

Concerning the air conditioner problem: Charlie would email his team members the minute the equipment broke, asking for any input or recommendations, and by the next business day he would have the authority to not only fix the problem, but to rebuild the entire air conditioning system on the shop floor.

How could this happen from just an email?

Well, the morning after the air conditioner broke, Charlie noticed two interesting emails. The first was from Phil Omman, Charlie's "boss," who was asking Charlie's permission to move ahead with an overhaul of the air conditioning and ventilation system at the plant. The second was from Lester Jocobs, Phil's boss, and the chief operating officer of Cissa, congratulating Charlie on his good work with his Line Empowerment Team and his "continued efforts to make Cissa a place where all employees contribute to the health of the company and to each other." Apparently, Phil had gotten Charlie's request and an important email from Lester Jacobs.

Jan Leiter, one of Charlie's line staff and a member of the Line Empowerment Team, had notified Jorge Muñoz, a facilities manager at Cissa's Houston plant of the air conditioning breakdown. Jan remembered meeting Jorge while in Texas for a three-day seminar on problem solving. At that seminar, Jan had learned that Jorge was an expert on air conditioning systems.

Jan, who had received Charlie's email while checking her email from home, emailed Jorge, asking him for any input he might have on the current problem.

When Jorge received the email from Jan, he remembered her talking about the troubled air conditioning system. He took the opportunity to share his knowledge of the problem and his recommendation for a solution to help his friend in need. In an email to Phil Omman and Lester Jacobs, Jorge outlined what he saw as a flaw in the design and structure of the air conditioning shafts at Charlie's plant. Using details of the plant that he gathered through the company's Intranet, he outlined what it would take to fix the problem once and for all. He knew that extra costs would have to be justified, so he included information from his research that showed how, over the course of three years, the new system would not only save money, but would increase productivity. His research showed that the new design would decrease the energy used to cool the plant and require much less repair work over the years. He also wrote about how his design would increase the circulation of air in the entire plant by 45% and give the line workers a much healthier working atmosphere. Jorge's plan would most likely translate into increased productivity and fewer accidents—not to mention a cooler break room.

Chief Operating Officer Jacobs used the situation to reward Charlie and his team for a job well done—for collaborating successfully to solve a real business need. He felt that it was an opportunity to reinforce the flow of communications that allowed for this solution to develop. His email praised Charlie, Charlie's Line Empowerment Team, Jan, and Jorge's efforts to do something for the good of the company. Lester also sent separate congratulations to Phil for acting as a facilitator and mentor to Charlie and encouraging Phil to put the power back in Charlie's hands by asking Charlie to "approve" the new plans for an air conditioning overhaul. Subsequently, employees got a message from Lester reminding them that the power to make the company a better place lies in every worker. Charlie, Jan, and Jorge were all commended in this message.

What does it take to create an atmosphere where this type of collaboration is possible?

THE LEARNING ORGANIZATION—
A COLLABORATIVE WORK ENVIRONMENT

Learning organizations spend a tremendous amount of time and money setting up the proper environment, building the best tools, and continuously training their employees in the proper skill sets to work collaboratively. The scope of their efforts is so great that it cannot be discussed in detail in this book. But most learning organizations work towards a culture where managers act as facilitators, not guardians or chiefs, and all employees:

- are given access to as much information as possible
- share information with other employees, key vendors, and suppliers
- possess the freedom, power, and tools to communicate openly
- openly express problems or concerns, and share successes
- make informed decisions on both an operational and strategic level
- seek to continuously improve their organization
- are encouraged to build lasting and personal relationships with others
- are valued as part of the organization's "family"
- are responsible to every other member of the organization

CHAPTER SUMMARY

- The Information Revolution has given birth to learning organizations—they rely on an empowered workforce, where employees have the information, tools, and training necessary to make important business decisions on their own.

- Teamwork, communication, and collaboration are essential to success in this environment.

- Whether you work for yourself, a large corporation, or a small business, chances are you will be in, or interact with, an organization that is, or is becoming, a learning organization, and if you can master the skills required to work well with others, you will succeed.

Skill Building

1. Find out your company's mission statement. How does this affect your work?
2. What characteristics of your company or work environment resemble a learning organization? How?
3. Do these characteristics enable you to work better, faster, or smarter? Or do they put additional pressure on you?
4. Are you part of a team? If so, is it a successful team? Why?

CHAPTER | 2

THE BENEFITS AND CHALLENGES OF WORKING IN TEAMS

LEARNING OBJECTIVES

After reading this chapter you should be able to:

- understand how working in teams can be more rewarding than working alone
- understand the challenges that come with working in teams
- point out three major benefits and three related potential challenges to working in teams

A DOUBLE-EDGED SWORD

With an emphasis on communication, teamwork, and problem solving, employees are being given more choices and more chances to succeed than ever before. However, with this opportunity comes additional responsibilities and more risk of failure.

What if, for example, your job was to sort all incoming mail into the appropriate department bins so that seven different delivery clerks, one from each department, could focus on delivery and not sorting. Under this scenario your job was very predictable and your tasks were clearly defined each and every day: consolidate incoming mail bins, sort mail by floor location and department, and then re-pack the mail into the department bins according to floor location. Your job was predictable, until recently, when your boss announced that there was good news and bad news due to the recent downsizing. The good news—you were not fired. The bad news—instead of a sorter and seven individual delivery clerks, there would be a total staff count of five and you would all be equal members of the Correspondence Delivery Team, and would, of course, be expected to continue to meet the 10:00 and 2:00 deadlines. (All mail that is delivered to your mailroom by 7:00 a.m. is to be on the desk of the recipient by 10:00 and all mail delivered to you before noon handed to each employee by 2:00 p.m.—deadlines hard enough to meet with eight employees!)

Now, rather than being responsible for your own production, and your own performance, you are sharing the responsibility for the entire delivery process with four other employees. Of course you are excited by the change and the challenge to meet the deadlines with a reduced staff, but you are also scared to death about having to worry about not only your own work, but the work of your teammates. You are not sure how the new team will work, how you will perform within this team, and how well the team will work as a unit.

In order for you to succeed in this scenario you must master effective communication skills and learn how to lead, motivate, and produce in a team environment. When you collaborate on important projects on a day-to-day basis with a diverse group of individuals, communication and team skills become extremely important for success. When working with others, whether in a formal or informal setting, you will find one thing for certain: You will be met with many challenges. However, overcoming those challenges will reward you with even more benefits than you could have achieved on your own.

TEAMS CAN OUTPERFORM INDIVIDUALS

When employees working in teams are effective, they are able to accomplish much more than their counterparts working on the same tasks individually. The synergy that can occur in successful teams, where the overall performance of the team is greater than the sum of the performance of all its participants, comes from three major factors: the accumulation of more knowledge, the inclusion of broader perspectives and multiple alternatives, and greater satisfaction and support from the members. Yet these benefits come with challenges as well.

Benefit: Better Informed Decisions

When important decisions must be made, it is often good practice to put a team on it. Teams can do a better job investigating the situation, gathering relevant information, devising multiple alternatives, and building a case for the best possible solution. Teams are better at doing these tasks because they can gather more information and they represent more knowledge than individuals working on the same problem separately. The diversity of members in a team leads to different perspectives and usually results in many alternative solutions. Teams tend to generate more quality ideas because of the diversity of its membership.

Challenge: Timeliness and Compromise

While the team setup may be excellent for developing alternative solutions and coming up with all the facts necessary to make a quality (informed) decision, the final decision is often made by an individual rather than the team. This is especially true when the decision must be made quickly, because the very same qualities that deliver superior results in idea formulation, multiple perspectives, and breadth of knowledge can be a killer in the decision-making process. Groups often work more slowly, especially when making decisions, because all those opinions and perspectives have to be heard. Also, groups tend to compromise when it comes time for the final solution—the best solution may offend some members or leave others out, and groups will compromise the end result in order to keep peace among themselves.

Benefit: Higher Levels of Commitment, Motivation, and Satisfaction

Individuals who participate in a team are more likely to be personally motivated to perform well—they exhibit a sense of duty towards their peers and take an ownership role in the team. Team members are also more likely to be satisfied with the decisions reached by the team because they all participated in formulating the decision, and they, therefore, feel they "own" the decision. Because team members are motivated and satisfied in the decision-making process, they tend to be more committed to the decision. Basically, by working in a team environment, individuals often feel better on a personal level about their work and their involvement within the team structure. Feeling good about work usually means that employees perform better, are more productive, and make fewer errors, all while requiring less formal supervision or management.

Challenge: Leadership and Unity

While commitment, motivation, and satisfaction are higher for members of effective teams, many teams are not effective. In order for a team to achieve high levels of effectiveness and for its members to be highly committed, motivated to perform, and satisfied with their involvement, leadership by one or several members of the team must be displayed. Too often teams, or any groups of employees, are dominated by power-hungry individuals or by cliques (sub-groups). When either a clique or a team member dominates the rest of the team, this can undermine the commitment, motivation, and satisfaction of the entire team and often hinders the accumulation of more knowledge, the inclusion of broader perspectives, and the generation of multiple alternatives.

Benefit: Rich Communication

When commitment, motivation, and satisfaction are high within a team, its members are more likely to build and maintain higher levels of trust. When trust is high, communication becomes richer. Rich communication is open and free-flowing. Members are not afraid to say what they mean and mean what they say. Creativity and expression are encouraged and the rewards include breakthrough ideas and one-of-a-kind solutions.

Challenge: *Groupthink*

Sometimes, when a group has been together for a long time and has grown accustomed to the ideas and feelings of each other to the point where they say and do things just to make each other happy, *groupthink* can occur. Groupthink undermines the creative process and doesn't encourage multiple solutions or different perspectives. Groupthink trades open communication and challenging viewpoints for ease-of-action.

Practice:

1. If you were the designated leader of a team at work, what would you do to encourage quality decisions?

2. How would you make sure commitment, unity, and satisfaction were high, while avoiding domination from a clique or from an overly aggressive member?

3. How would you avoid groupthink?

Answers:

You could ensure commitment, unity, and quality decision-making within your team by making sure the team works in an atmosphere that encourages respect for each other's ideas, opinions, and points of view. You also would want to make sure that every member's voice is heard—even if you have to drag it out. It is important for you, as the leader, to set the tone and involve everyone in discussions. You can avoid negative compromises by challenging the group to come up with optimum solutions, even if it means that some members' ideas are not used, as long as your actions are respectful to all members. You could avoid groupthink by either appointing someone as the *devil's advocate* to really challenge every idea or by bringing in an outsider to present views or opinions that differ from those of the team. Bringing in an outsider will introduce fresh ideas into the team and certainly help avoid groupthink.

CHAPTER SUMMARY

- Teamwork can be more challenging than working individually, but it can also be more rewarding and more productive
- Effective teams can outperform individuals working on the same tasks because they:
  - can make better, more informed decisions by accumulating more knowledge, including broader perspectives and developing multiple alternative solutions
  - encourage rich communication, which invites creativity and fosters one-of-a-kind solutions
  - maintain higher levels of commitment, motivation, and satisfaction
- Teams can also be challenging because:
  - decisions take longer to make and may require compromises that lead to inferior solutions
  - they require leaders to ensure unity, commitment, and motivation
  - can lead to groupthink where members merely go along with ideas that won't rock the boat, leading to very little creativity and lackluster performance

Skill Building

1. In chapter one's Skill Building exercise you were asked if you were part of a successful team:

   List at least five benefits that come from being a part of that team.

Benefits:

1. _____   2. _____

3. _____   4. _____

5. _____

Now list any challenges that you have encountered due to your membership on this team:

Challenges:

1. _____

2. _____

3. _____

4. _____

PART II

COMMUNICATING EFFECTIVELY WITH OTHERS

Part II will give you the skills and knowledge you need to communicate effectively with others. You will learn about the process of communication and how to use your knowledge of the audience and subject to effectively send messages that are clearly understood. You will learn about how different points of view must be considered in order to understand the communication needs of audience.

Chapters five through eight will help you become a more effective business communicator—giving you the ability to say what you mean when you write or talk. You will also find helpful tips for building your listening skills and successfully participating in meetings. Finally, you will be able to look for common barriers to effective communication and overcome any hurdles that are in your way.

CHAPTER | 3

THE COMMUNICATION PROCESS

LEARNING OBJECTIVES

After reading this chapter you should be able to:

- identify and understand the elements in the process of communication

- identify the personal and environmental factors that contribute to an individual's perspective and understand how perspective affects the communication process

IT'S NOT AS EASY AS *ONE, TWO, THREE*

How many times have you thought you understood exactly what your boss, colleague, wife, or friend wanted from you, only to find out after hours of hard work that, to your surprise, you had done something wrong? You probably replied, "But that's not what you said" or "I thought you wanted . . . [something else]." Chances are that somewhere, somehow, someone wasn't communicating effectively.

The ability to communicate effectively is one of the most important skills required to work successfully with others. Without communication, you really can't accomplish much. Even though you may communicate with others on a daily basis, you rarely think about the complexities of the communication process itself. Yet understanding the process and its components is key to improving your communication skills.

COMMUNICATION AS A PROCESS

We can define communication as follows:

> Communication is a process undertaken by two or more individuals in which messages are exchanged and understood.

For each message, there are at least two individuals required: a sender and a receiver. The sender is the individual attempting to send a message or express a thought or emotion to someone else. The receiver is the "someone else"—the person to whom the message is sent. Usually, when the receiver receives a message, he sends a message back to the sender acknowledging the receipt of the message. This is called *feedback*. Of course, in any communication, both parties are actively involved in sending and receiving messages and, likewise, feedback is also a two-way process.

While the sending and receiving actions are an obvious part of the communication process, there are other elements that are not so obvious. Before sending any messages, the sender first:

- formulates her ideas about the topic, then
- proceeds to process all sorts of information relating to the topic of the intended message and the receiver, and finally
- composes a message.

These steps make up the mental process known as *encoding*. Likewise, the receiver goes through a similar process. The receiver:

- translates the message, then

- formulates his/her own ideas about the message, and then

- composes a response or feedback.

The translation and idea formulation on the part of the receiver is often called *decoding*. Most of the coding and decoding takes place in the subconscious, which means you often are not even aware that it is taking place.

Once the message is ready to be sent, it needs a medium, or a way to get from one person to another. This element of the communication process is called the *channel*. The communication channel is the medium that the message travels through to get from the sender to the receiver. The most common channels used in business are letters, emails, memos, reports, proposals, telephone calls, and face to face discussions. With today's sophisticated communications technology there are also hybrids—channels that mix the above. An example of a hybrid would be a videoconference where individuals can see and hear each other while also working on a written document together. Whatever channel is used has a major impact on the communication process because it determines what type of message will be formulated. More will be discussed regarding channels and effective use of different channels in chapters five and 12.

The following is a visual representation of the communication process.

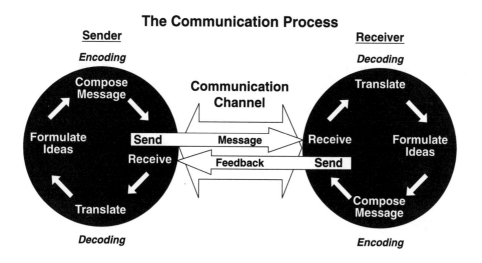

The Communication Process

Practice:

1. You are waiting to deposit your check and are next in line for an available teller at the bank. At what point in the communication process are you? Can you get to the teller without first being a receiver?

2. On your way to the water cooler you notice a new employee tipping his head to you. You respond with a smile and a nod of your head. According to the definition of communication in this chapter, did you and your new colleague communicate? Who was the receiver and who was the sender?

Answers:

1. You are waiting for a message from an available teller and are in receiver mode. You may receive a clue from the environment that a teller will be ready when you notice that a customer vacates his/her spot from the teller window. This will heighten your senses, as you await the official message—a *bing* as an arrow lights up pointing you to the teller, or a smile and a friendly 'Next,' from the available teller. You cannot get to an available teller without first being a receiver— something has to signal you to go.

2. Yes, according the definition of communication in this chapter you and your new colleague did engage in and understand the exchange of messages. Messages involved in communication do not have to be verbal. Actually, in communications involving selling and negotiations, non-verbal communications play a key role. In this scenario, your colleague was the initiator of the communication and your message in response was feedback, so the colleague was the sender, and you were the receiver.

IMPORTANT FACTORS THAT AFFECT THE COMMUNICATION PROCESS

There are many important factors that affect the communication process such as whether the sender and receiver speak the same language, read on the same level, both have computers, etc. The most important factors that affect the communication process can be grouped into two categories: environmental and personal.

Environmental Factors

The environment affects the communication process by introducing outside factors into the process and often creating *noise*. Noise usually complicates the process by making it difficult to decode messages. However, sometimes environmental factors can serve to facilitate the communication process. There are also times when they may stop communication altogether.

Environmental factors include the weather, the temperature, the time, other people, media, and of course, external facilities such as meeting rooms, phones, computers, etc.

Now, to understand how external factors can affect the communication process, read the following example: Imagine you are on the phone with your spouse discussing the possibility of leaving work early in order to see your daughter's first ballet recital and your boss happens to walk by and hear the conversation. Instead of ignoring you, or even giving you a reprimand for making a personal call, she tells you that your daughter's recital is obviously very important to you and gives you permission to leave an hour early. Doesn't this help you communicate your plans more effectively with your spouse?

However, imagine you are trying to close a big deal on the phone and the rest of your office is having a birthday party, complete with raucous singing and hefty laughter. Doesn't this make your communication effort a challenge?

Think of the last time you tried to talk to a friend or family member on the phone and the line was busy. How did this environmental factor affect your communication?

Personal Factors

When encoding and decoding messages in the communication process, individual, historical and practical factors affect your coding decisions. These factors are considered personal. Individual factors include your:

- age
- gender
- primary language
- attitude/style
- emotions

Historical factors that affect communication include your:

- rearing (family upbringing)
- education
- experiences (personal and work-related)

Practical personal factors include your current:

- skills
- abilities
- knowledge (re: topic, audience, channels, etc.)

CHAPTER SUMMARY

- In order to work well with others you need to communicate effectively.
- Understanding the communication process is a key to becoming an effective communicator.
- Communication is a process undertaken by two or more individuals in which messages are exchanged and understood.
- Both environmental and personal factors affect the communication process.

Skill Building

Think of a topic or subject that you frequently discuss at work as part of your job.
Briefly describe the topic:

Now think of the individual, historical, and practical factors that affect how you think about this topic.

Fill in the blank in this question with each of the personal factors listed on page 28 and jot down your answers to all eleven questions.

Key Questions:

Does your _____ affect how you feel about this topic?

How does this feeling change the way you see and talk about the subject?

CHAPTER | 4

DIFFERENT POINTS OF VIEW

LEARNING OBJECTIVES

After reading this chapter you should be able to:

- evaluate your perspectives and understand how they affect your communication efforts

- empathize with your audience, or the person(s) to whom you are communicating

- evaluate the perspective of your audience and analyze how any difference between your perspective and theirs will affect the communication effort

PERSONAL FACTORS AND PERSPECTIVE

All of the personal factors covered in the last chapter affect how you think and, therefore, how you communicate by influencing your perspective and shaping your reality. Your perspective guides the way you see things or make sense of them, and is based on your evaluation of each situation in relation to your past experiences—including all of the factors listed in the last chapter.

A definition of perspective:

Perspective: a point of view or position from which a person sees experiences or understands another person, place, or thing; a mental picture from which a person determines the relative importance of things.

Every individual has a unique perspective or "point of view" about everything in their world. Different people may have different perspectives about the same thing. Imagine that you are wearing glasses tinted green and your friend is wearing shades tinted pink. Everything that you and your friend look at appears totally different, even though you are looking at the same thing. Now imagine that you and your friend tried to explain what you saw to a third friend, without letting on that you were wearing different colored glasses. Do you think that your friend would get the same message and mental picture from both of you? Are either of you wrong in your description? Would the friend you are describing this image to be confused?

Obviously, perspective plays a key role in the communication process. How can you develop a message that doesn't reflect your perspective on the subject? Conversely, how can you translate a message—decode it—without considering your perspective on the subject?

Practice:

Imagine that you attend a seminar entitled *Personal Power: Getting in Touch with the Real You*, because your friend wanted to go and wouldn't go alone. Although you attend the seminar, reluctant at first, you find it to be an incredibly effective workshop because it helps you to realize what really "makes you tick." During the seminar, the speaker outlines many of the personal factors described in the last chapter, and she helps you to understand how key events in your life have shaped your current perspectives and your self-worth. She also conducts several exercises that help you build the skills necessary to create new perspectives when they would be advantageous for you. For instance, she shows you a method that gives you specific instructions to determine whether your perspective on a particular issue is a positive (empowering) perspective, or a negative (limiting) perspective. She then teaches you how to shift your perspective if it is limiting. When you understand this message, you immediately think of three instances back at your job where you could have exercised this technique and solved important problems with your boss.

After realizing that the seminar you attended was transformational—it changed the way you think and will behave—you feel like it is your mission to get as many people at your job to attend the same seminar. You personally feel that if your colleagues could learn to do these empowering exercises, the office would be a better place and the company would be much better off.

Now, consider how this experience would affect your ability to communicate. Let's say you had to submit a one-page essay to your boss describing the benefits of the seminar, how it would help you on the job, and why the company should pay for your attendance.

Questions to Consider:

1. Would your essay to your boss be more convincing before or after attending the seminar?

2. How would it differ?

3. How would your boss view the different requests?

4. Does your experience affect what you say? How you say it?

Answers and explanations:

1. Your essay would surely be much more convincing after your experience—after you attended the seminar.

2. Your attitude and emotions about the seminar would be much more positive and your skills, ability, and knowledge regarding the content of the seminar and its practical applications on the job would be much more complete after attending the seminar. Your ability to concretely describe the benefits of the seminar, and use examples, would surely change the style and content of the essay.

3. Your boss would be more engaged by the letter that you would write after attending the seminar. Using concrete examples of how the tools you learned at the seminar would directly affect your performance on the job would have a much larger impact on your boss than merely listing benefits as they appear on the marketing brochure describing the seminar.

4. Yes, your experience gives you concrete details, and real-life examples to use in your letter, and your emotional involvement provides alternative and richer ways to describe your experience. How you say it will reflect your positive emotions. You would use more declarative phrases and more exclamation points. The tone would be more positive and the energy level would surely be much higher.

UNDERSTANDING YOUR OWN PERSPECTIVES

In order to communicate effectively with others, it is important to examine and understand your own perspectives. Knowing how your personal experiences, knowledge, skills, attitudes, and emotions affect your unique perspective in any given situation will help you to recognize the differences in perspective between you and others. This will, in turn, help you to bridge the gap from a communications standpoint and deliver an effective message.

Whether you realize it or not, every situation that involves communication requires you to make a decision regarding your point of view. Before you encode or decode a message, you check your *reality bank*, the place where you store all the data that make up your perspectives. To be an effective communicator, you must be aware of this process and of the influence that your personal factors have on your perspectives, and in turn, the influence your perspective has on your ideas about any given person, place, or thing.

As a helpful tool you can repeat and follow the advice of these phrases every time you enter into a discussion or begin to write a document:

- I will seek to understand my feelings and ideas about this topic before I communicate anything about it.

- I will seek to understand my feeling and ideas about this person before I communicate anything with/to them.

Practice:

The following questions can be used to analyze any given topic or situation in order for you to better understand how your personal perspective may be *coloring* the way you see (and therefore communicate) it.

Find your last letter, memo, or business proposal, or think about the last serious discussion you had with someone at work and try to answer the following questions.

Checking Your Perspective

Regarding the topic:

1. What is the topic?

2. How do I feel about this topic? Positive or negative? Explain why.

3. Am I comfortable with my current knowledge, skills, and ability relating to this topic in order to discuss it the way I want?

4. Are there any historical or emotional issues that affect the way I think about this topic? What is the effect that these issues have on my view of the topic?

5. Can I take a neutral position on this topic if I have to? In other words, can I put my feelings and emotions aside regarding this topic and deal with it on a purely objective level?

6. Will my feelings about this topic affect my ability to effectively discuss it, even if others don't share the same feelings I have about it?

Regarding the person you are communicating with:

1. Who is this person?

2. How do I feel about this person? Positive or negative? Explain why.

3. Am I comfortable with my current knowledge, skills, and ability relating to this person in order to communicate effectively with him/her?

4. Are there any historical or emotional issues that affect the way I think about him/her? What is the effect that these issues have on my view of this person?

5. Can I communicate with a neutral attitude with this person? In other words, can I put my personal feelings and emotions about this person aside and deal with him/her on a purely objective level?

6. Will my feelings about this person affect my ability to effectively communicate with him/her, even if he/she doesn't feel the same about me?

Answering these questions every time you make an effort to communicate with someone may not be practical or possible. However, the more you ask these questions, the easier it will become for you to understand your perspective, and this will be a tremendous help in communicating effectively.

RESPECT OTHER POINTS OF VIEW

It is also important to evaluate the perspective of your audience before you begin communicating. Since you probably work with a diverse group of people who all bring different backgrounds, experiences, cultures, and perspectives with them, communication can often be difficult, especially if you are not aware of these differences. However, understanding that diversity requires a special awareness should give you a professional and personal advantage in your communication efforts, and help you in your career and in your life.

If you are unable to appreciate their perspective, then respect the fact that they are entitled to their own opinions and beliefs. Particularly when you are working with a diverse group of people, you must respect that others will have different opinions, beliefs, expectations, and values than you. You show respect for others by treating their opinions, beliefs, and behaviors by withholding judgement and ridicule. Just because others do things differently than you does not mean that they are wrong or bad. In any case, try to view the topic or situation from their perspective, as well as your own, and you will find that it is much easier to communicate with them.

Understanding through Empathy

Getting to know the person with whom you are communicating is very important. Knowing where they come from and what attitudes and perspectives they bring to the conversation can be very important for effective communication. Knowing their perspectives and biases will help you to send the right messages and help you better understand the messages they are sending to you.

The best way to understand someone who is not like you is to empathize with them. Empathy means that you try to share the same feelings with the other person. You make believe that you are in their shoes and try to think like them. The best way to do this is to ask empathic questions.

For instance, if you are meeting a colleague to work on a budget request for a new project and you can sense that your colleague is upset with your boss because of his attitude and particular behavior, you may want to ask empathic questions to find out more about his emotions so you can better communicate with him.

Some empathic questions would be:

- Are you allright?

- Is something bothering you?

- What is eating at you?

- Are you upset with the boss because . . . ?

- How come you always get so emotional with the boss when it comes to . . . ?

The more you know about each other's perspective, the better you will be able to communicate. Be careful: It is not always appropriate to probe this deeply. Before asking such personal questions of someone, think of whether you would be offended if that person asked you the same question. If you wouldn't be offended, then chances are, they won't either. If your questions are made in good faith, then you should be O.K. asking them.

CHAPTER SUMMARY

- Your personal factors shape your perspective, and your perspective plays a key role in determining how you will process information—both in encoding and decoding messages.

- By consciously evaluating your perspectives, you can begin to understand how they will affect your communication efforts.

- Effective communication begins by:

1. understanding your own perspective on the topic and the audience

2. showing empathy by seeking to understand the perspective of your audience (the person[s] you are communicating with), and

3. respecting their perspective, or at least respecting the difference between your perspective and theirs.

Skill Building

Use the Checking Your Perspective questions in the practice exercise earlier in the chapter and apply it to at least five communications during business tomorrow. Note how your different perspectives affect your communications.

CHAPTER | 5

SAYING WHAT YOU MEAN

LEARNING OBJECTIVES

After reading this chapter you should be able to:

- discuss the five basic elements of any message
- identify the topic, purpose, and audience of any message
- draft an effective message using a style that is sharp, formal, logical, and timely

EVERY MESSAGE HAS FIVE BASIC ELEMENTS

Typically, when you communicate with others, especially at work, it is usually for a specific reason and often follows a model or accepted standard. However, even if your message follows a standard it is still your message and how you choose to put your ideas into words will have a big impact on whether others get your point. In order to say what you mean, you need to consider these five basic elements of any message:

1. subject matter
2. audience
3. purpose
4. format
5. style

Subject Matter

The subject matter of your message is the specific topic that will be covered in the message. If you are writing to communicate a new policy or procedure at work, then that policy is the subject matter.

Why is the subject matter important?

Your knowledge of the subject matter will influence your perspective. How well you know the subject matter will certainly affect how well you can communicate about it. Can you speak or write about it as an expert? Or do you feel you are a novice? Are you comfortable with the subject? Does it cause any unusual feelings when you think about this subject? Once you answer these questions, then you can begin to think about how the subject will affect your audience. Do they know enough about the subject to understand what you will be saying? Are they experts on the subject? Are there any special considerations because of the subject matter? Will it cause any emotional response that you should be aware of?

Clearly, the subject matter has an effect on both the sender and receiver of the message, so it is important that you are aware of any significant effects it may have on the communication process.

Audience

What you say and how you say it depends upon your target audience. You must ask yourself: Who will receive this communication? Why? How important is this information to them? What special language/content considerations must I make based on my understanding of their perspective? Are there others that might see this message also? As we mentioned in the previous chapter, the more you know about your audience—about their perspectives, ideas, culture, etc.—the better able you will be to tailor your message to their communication needs.

When you send a message at work you will always have a very specific, targeted audience. Whether it is one person, an entire office, or the whole company, it is usually an audience that for one reason or another has an interest in your message because of the purpose and subject matter.

Purpose

One of the keys to saying what you mean is making sure that your message has a clearly stated purpose. When you communicate at work, you are not trying to entertain or to impress; your message has a purpose and should express an idea that will address a business issue as efficiently as possible. Your audience should not have to spend time reading between the lines or guessing at what you are trying to say. Your audience should know as quickly and as clearly as possible why your are sending them a message and what they need to do about it. This means that before you begin to draft your message, you need to be absolutely clear about your purpose.

Getting Started

Before you communicate an important message, whether it is writing a letter or memo, making an important phone call, or going to a meeting, you should do the following exercise to focus on your audience and your purpose.

Brainstorming

Stretch your biggest muscle, your brain, before drafting an important message by doing the following:

- Jot down ideas about what you want to say and how you might say it.

- Create a list of ideas to work with—no idea is too crazy for this list.

- List as many ways of expressing what you think is important as you can.

S.A.P. Query

Before drafting your message answer the following questions about your Subject Matter, your Audience, and the Purpose of your message:

1. Who is the primary audience? (Who will definitely receive this communication?)

2. Who is the secondary audience? (Who else might read this communication?)

3. What should this message accomplish? (What is its purpose?)

Try to pick a verb that describes the action of your message and then name the object of that action. If there is a receiver of the action name them too. The following table gives a few examples of how this works.

PURPOSE	ACTION	OBJECT OF THAT ACTION	RECEIVER OF THAT ACTION
explain a new policy to your office staff	to explain	the new policy	the office staff
remind a customer of a past due balance	to remind	a balance that is past due	your customer

Here are some verbs you might find helpful for describing the purpose of your message:

claim	enlist	remind	show
congratulate	explain	report	suggest
convince	identify	reprimand	summarize
correct	inform	request	urge
demand	praise	review	warn
demonstrate	propose	sell	welcome

4. What *should* happen as a result of this message?

5. What information *must* this communication include?

6. What additional information *could* this communication include?

By answering these important questions regarding the subject matter, the audience, and the purpose of your message, you can help ensure that it does exactly what it's supposed to do.

Practice:

Answer the five S.A.P. questions for the following scenarios.

Scenario 1. You are in charge of writing and sending the invitations to the birthday party for your boss.

Who will you send this invitation to?
Who else might see it?
What should this invitation do?
What information must it include?
What additional information could it include?

Scenario 2. You have discovered that the office cleaners that you hired several months ago have been slacking off lately and have even missed a few offices, including a key conference room. You must give them a warning and get them back on track before your company's vice president visits next week.

Who will receive this warning?
Who else might see it?
What should this communication do?
What information must it include?
What additional information could this include?

Possible Answers:

Scenario 1.

Who will you send this invitation to? Any employees, customers, or friends of the boss that the person arranging the party sees fit to invite.

Who else might see it? Your boss and possibly friends of the people you invite.

What should this invitation do? As its title indicates, this should invite people to your boss's party.

What information must it include? It must include the date, time, and location of the party.

What additional information could it include? It may include whether the recipient should bring a gift, directions, or any other incidental information regarding the party such as *bring your favorite party games* or *bring your favorite tapes or CDs*, etc.

Scenario 2.

Who will receive this warning? Probably the manager of the cleaning company and your boss.

Who else might see it? The people who do the cleaning and possibly others in your office.

What should this communication do? It should warn the company that the current behavior is unacceptable.

What information must it include? Details about the current behavior, including why it is unacceptable, how the job should be done, and when the task should be finished.

What additional information could this include? You may mention the information about the visit from your vice president and you may also give an ultimatum such as "if the job is not done to perfection tomorrow your company will lose our account, effective immediately."

Format

In this chapter, format refers to the form or channel that your communication will *travel*.

The most common written formats include letters, email, memos, reports, and proposals, while the most common formats for oral communication include face-to-face meetings, telephone calls, presentations, and videoconferences.

These common types of business communications often have predefined guidelines for their presentation. In other words, how they are laid out is often a standard that is set by the company or office that you work in.

Typically, most important business communications are done in writing so that there is a permanent record. Even if important information is relayed via a face-to-face meeting, a telephone call, or a videoconference, there are usually written notes, a published agenda, or a follow-up memo or letter—in order to document what was discussed.

When choosing a format for your message, you will need to consider your audience and your purpose. For instance, if you are sending a message that is considered very important, you will probably use a face-to-face meeting and support it with a report or an agenda and follow it up with a letter or memo. However, if you are passing some minor information to someone who needs it immediately, you might simply phone them or email them. Also, if the message that you will be delivering will require feedback in order for you to deliver it effectively, then you will probably go see the person or you will telephone him. Email often works for messages that require quick feedback.

Style

While styles may differ according to your own preferences, your knowledge of your audience, the subject matter, and the purpose and format of your message, most effective workplace communications share four common style traits: sharpness, attention to formality, logic, and attention to time.

Sharpness

Effective messages are sharp; they are specific, relevant, accurate, and complete yet concise. Include as many details and facts as possible to prevent vagueness, but keep the message relevant to the audience. Accuracy ensures that the communication is as authentic and reliable as possible, while completeness aims at giving the receiver everything he or she needs to comprehend the message and its meaning. Remember, however, that in business time is money and no one should have to wade through unnecessary rhetoric to get to the meat of the message—be succinct in explaining your purpose and delivering the key information.

Attention to Formality

Effective messages convey their meaning with the proper formality for the intended audience. Very formal communications can be described as proper, stuffy, or distanced. If you were writing a letter to the president of your union, or the CEO of your company, you would write it in the most formal style. Very informal communications make heavy use of slang and colloquialisms—not the language spoken for business. Very informal is how you converse with your friends at a baseball game. Most messages fall in the middle of this scale, slightly on the formal side.

Logic

Effective messages are easily understood because they follow a logical or rational path. Use rational arguments that demonstrate the meaning of your message and, when possible, use sequential steps that help the audience get to the point of understanding one piece of information at a time.

Attention to Time

Effective messages are sent on time. If the information is needed immediately, then send the message now. Receivers also need to know when you need their feedback or other follow-up activities. If you need a response immediately, you have to make it clear in your message. Use specific times and dates when applicable.

CHAPTER SUMMARY

- All messages have five basic elements:

  - Audience • Subject Matter • Purpose • Format • Style

- Each of these elements affects what you say and how you say it.

- Before you communicate you should outline key ideas and answers to important questions on your subject matter, your audience, and the purpose of your message.

- You should be familiar with the format choices for business communications.

- When communicating at work, your style should be sharp (specific, relevant, accurate, and complete), appropriately formal, logical, and time-specific.

Skill Building

Take the most recent communication you received at work and critique it against what you now know about effective messages.

1. Is the message effective? Did the sender do the necessary work to construct an effective message?
2. Can you easily understand the topic and the purpose?
3. Is the format appropriate to the message?
4. Is the writing sharp (specific, relevant, accurate, and complete)?
5. Was it timely? Does it give you a time-frame for any follow-up activities?
6. How could you make it better?

Now take the last communication that you sent to someone at work and critique it against what you now know about effective messages.

1. Is the message effective? Did you do the necessary work to construct an effective message?
2. Can you easily understand the topic and the purpose?
3. Is the format appropriate to the message?
4. Is the writing sharp (specific, relevant, accurate, and complete)?
5. Was it timely? Did you give a time-frame for any follow-up activities?
6. How could you make it better?

CHAPTER | 6

DELIVERING POSITIVE MESSAGES WITH POWER

LEARNING OBJECTIVES

After reading this chapter you should be able to:

- say what you mean when you have to convey a positive or neutral message
- remind, request, respond, and thank with confidence and professionalism

THE MOST COMMON BUSINESS MESSAGES

Most business communications are about business. Yet, the messages you send on a day-to-day basis vary in content and purpose. However, if you are like most people, many of your messages will have a similar purpose. This chapter covers tips for saying what you mean when:

- informing or reminding
- requesting or inquiring
- following up or responding
- thanking, welcoming, or congratulating

GENERAL TIPS FOR CONVEYING A POSITIVE OR NEUTRAL MESSAGE

Many of the everyday tasks that you will perform on the job include reminding, requesting, responding, thanking, welcoming, and congratulating others. When your purpose in a message is to convey a positive or neutral message, three basic strategies are important for saying what you mean. They include:

- clarifying your purpose
- choosing the proper tone of voice
- providing all the necessary information

Clarifying Your Purpose

It should come as no surprise that your purpose should be clear, since this is the case for any good message. To clarify your purpose, turn it into a topic sentence, which can serve as the introduction to your message.

Here's an example:

Purpose:	to congratulate Elizabeth on her new contract extension.
Topic Sentence:	Please accept my sincerest congratulations regarding your recent contract extension.

Choose the Proper Tone of Voice

Be sure to use the proper tone of voice. This means that you need to think about your audience and specifically the relationship between you and your audience.

An important question to ask:

- Is this going to a superior, a subordinate, or a co-worker (an equal)?

If the message is going to a client or a customer, ask yourself:

- Is this message coming from me personally or am I a spokesperson for my company?
- Is the communication a message to the individual or will it be interpreted to apply to his/her entire organization?

When sending a message to a superior, make sure you are more formal and show respect in your tone of voice. A message to a subordinate should be somewhat formal and should show respect as well. When sending a message to a colleague, however, you don't have to be as formal.

The following table briefly shows how even an email heading can have a different tone depending on the relationship between the sender and the recipient.

RELATIONSHIP BETWEEN PARTIES	EMAIL SUBJECT LINE AND FIRST LINE OF MESSAGE
Co-workers To: Janice Caine, Manager From: Clive Jerrod, Manager	**RE: Go Indians!** Word on the street says the big cheese wants you in Cleveland . . .
Subordinate to Superior To: Carl Lepone, Senior VP From: Janice Caine, Manager	**RE: Questions regarding a rumor about my job?** Carl, It has come to my attention through a rumor circulating in our department that I will be reassigned to Cleveland . . .
Superior to Subordinate To: Janice Caine, Manager From: Carl Lepone, Senior VP	**RE: Rumor regarding Cleveland . . .** Janice, regarding this rumor about your re-assignment to Cleveland, let's talk ASAP . . .

Provide All the Necessary Information

Don't omit any important information. Even if your purpose is clearly stated and your tone is perfect, you may not get the results you are hoping for if you forget to include important information. Remember to brainstorm ahead of time and use the S.A.P. query from chapter five to help you.

TIPS FOR SPECIFIC POSITIVE OR NEUTRAL MESSAGES

Informing or Reminding

If you are composing a message that aims to inform or remind, follow this strategy:

1. Tell your audience what you're going to tell them: In other words, include an introduction that gives the recipient of your message the purpose, right at the beginning of the message.
2. Tell them: Provide the specific information you need to convey.
3. Tell them why you told them: Indicate why this information is important.

Requesting or Inquiring

When your message is a request or inquiry, it is good practice to follow the same general format as communications that inform or remind.

1. Tell them what you're going to tell them: Outline the general nature of your request.
2. Tell them: Make the request in a kind, yet professional manner. Be detailed so the recipient knows exactly what you want.
3. Tell them why you told them: Explain why and when you need it.
4. Thank them: No one is obligated to give you anything. People are far more likely to give you what you want if you are gracious and thankful.

Practice A:

Imagine that you are Anthony, an associate editor. On a separate sheet of paper use the formula above to write your boss an email requesting next week off. Your wife just had a baby and you have plenty of vacation days to cover 10 days. You have arranged for your colleague, Moira, to cover for you in case of any emergencies and she has your home number, just in case.

Following Up or Responding:

1. Begin by thanking the person.

2. Remind the person of your last communication: Give them highlights of the request so that there is nothing vague about what was asked of whom.

3. Provide them with the information they requested and/or explain why you can't give them what they wanted.

4. End on the assumption that you will continue working together by using a *looking forward* type of statement.

Thanking, Welcoming, and Congratulating

When writing a thank you, a welcoming, or a congratulating message, it is best to follow the *tell them what you're going to tell them, tell them, tell them why you told them* model, making certain that you are:

- Brief and sincere: too much flattery can be construed as insincere.

- On time: if its not, it won't mean a thing.

- Specific about what you are thankful for/welcoming the person to/congratulating the person for: Use exact names, dates, places, etc.

- Personal: Explain why you are grateful/what the persons' arrival will mean for you/what the event means to you.

Practice B:

Imagine you are the boss, Alice (from Practice A). On a separate sheet of paper, use the appropriate formulas to respond to Anthony's request for a vacation next week.

CHAPTER SUMMARY

- When conveying a positive or neutral message the general formula for saying what you mean is to:

  1. State your general purpose.
  2. Provide specific details.
  3. Explain the importance of what you've said.
  4. Express thanks.

- It is also important to use the proper tone.

Skill Building

Pay particular attention to the brief messages that you are a part of over the next 24 hours and note whether they are informing, requesting, thanking, or congratulating. Take note as to whether or not they follow the general and specific formulas in this chapter. If you find that your messages are not following these rules, *stop everything* and make a conscious effort to follow the advice in this chapter on your next positive or neutral message.

Possible Answers to Practice Exercises:

Practice A

Alice:

I am emailing you to request the next two weeks off. I would like to take my vacation days starting next week, on Monday, February 13th and continuing through Friday, the 24th. My wife gave birth to our son, Lukas, last night, and I will be helping her with the baby and around the house, as she settles into her new role as mother.

I have arranged for Moira to cover any emergencies while I am gone, and she knows to call me at home if necessary.

Mommy and baby are doing fine and should be home Saturday.

Thanks again for your flexibility.

Anthony

Practice B

Anthony:

I am emailing you to congratulate you on the new addition to your family and to let you know that your request for vacation has been granted. Of course you can have the next two weeks off—you deserve the break—and what better way to spend it than with your wife and new child.

I will meet with Moira and make sure that she is ready for any emergency that comes up—I would hate to have to bother you or the baby.

Hope mommy, daddy, and baby are all doing well.

Looking forward to meeting your new son, Lukas!

Alice

CHAPTER | 7

TIPS FOR CONVEYING BAD OR NEGATIVE NEWS

LEARNING OBJECTIVES

After reading this chapter you should be able to:

- say what you mean when you have to convey a negative or unpleasant message
- complain, correct, reject, or demand in a professional and courteous manner

CONVEYING A NEGATIVE OR UNPLEASANT MESSAGE

Unfortunately you will have to communicate bad news from time to time. When conveying a negative or unpleasant message you can still communicate effectively and professionally by following the tips in this chapter, which will help you say what you mean when:

- complaining

- correcting or adjusting

- rejecting or refusing

- reminding or demanding

When conveying a negative or unpleasant message you should follow these general guidelines:

- Always respect your audience

  — When you have to convey a message that the recipient surely does not want to receive, how you say it will determine whether or not you maintain a positive relationship.

  — Bad news must, therefore, be delivered tactfully and respectfully, using words that show you gave careful thought to the situation.

- Avoid abusive language or tone

  — Keep your emotions in check.

  — Avoid insults or attacks.

  — Remember that the message should be a professional communication of specific information, not a tool for you to release your frustrations. If the message is too emotional and includes insults, you will not be advancing your cause and you will be doing a disservice to your organization.

- Be reasonable and very specific

  — Make sure the complaint and the action you are requesting match the nature of the problem.

- Use *I* and not *you*

  — People tend to be defensive when you attack them with *you*'s

  — Deflect the attack by using *I* instead of *you*

- Leave the door open for future communications

  — As a professional, you never know when you may encounter the same person in the future, so make sure you leave the door open for future interactions.

- End on a positive note

  — It is always good practice to end an otherwise negative exchange on a positive note, even if it is a minor note.

Tips for Specific Negative or Unpleasant Messages

Complaining

When delivering a message to complain about something, it is best to follow the *tell them* formula, specifically telling them:

1. What product, service, or item you are complaining about—be exact

2. What is/was wrong with the product, service or item—be as precise as possible

3. How the problem inconvenienced you or your company

4. What you want done to correct the problem or rectify the situation

5. When you need a response.

Also, don't forget to follow these guidelines for complaint messages:

- Don't be abusive

- Be reasonable

- Use *I* instead of *you*

  — For example, instead of saying, "The sandwich you delivered was not what I ordered," say, "I didn't get the sandwich that I ordered."

- Leave the door open

  — Don't say you will "never" do business with them again or anything to that effect, because they will surely not respond to you if you openly state that you are closing the door on them.

Correcting and Adjusting

If you are the one responding to a complaint, here are a few guidelines to help you say what you mean:

- Apologize, but don't be overly apologetic or desperate sounding.

- Be specific about exactly how you will correct the problem or why you can't do anything about it.

- Be specific about exactly what happened to cause the problem.

- If it was something that they did, don't be abusive and make sure that you include a suggestion that ensures it doesn't happen again.

  — For example, you could mention, " . . . and in the future, please be sure to include both your account number and your purchase order number when you phone your order in."

- Avoid absolutes

  — Stay away from rhetoric such as, "This will never happen again."

- End on a positive note.

  — You can include positive endings that leave the door open such as, " . . . and we look forward to your continued business," or "We value your business."

Practice A:

It is Saturday evening and you are steaming mad. You cancelled plans to spend the day doing something you really enjoy because your cable company was supposed to install a new box in your new den. They were scheduled to be at your house between noon and five p.m. and you waited all afternoon for them but they never showed. In fact, they never even called. You called their customer service line at 5:15 only to find out that they don't offer customer service after five on Saturdays and they are closed Sundays. You did get a fax number and you are sitting down at your computer now, to draft a fax. Use the guidelines covered so far in this chapter and write that fax.

REJECTING AND REFUSING

When you have to reject or refuse someone, be prompt: You will ease their pain and increase the chances that the relationship will stay professional between you and the recipient. Waiting for an extended length of time before you reject or refuse someone just because it is unpleasant for you is unprofessional and only makes things worse for the recipient, since their expectations continue to mount each day they don't hear from you.

In addition, follow these suggestions:

1. Begin by thanking the person for offering their services.

2. State something positive about them.

— You might tell a job applicant who was rejected, "We were impressed by your resume . . . ."

3. Be firm and clear in your rejection without being harsh.

— Continuing the example from above, " . . . however, we are currently unable to off you a position at this time" works much better than, ". . . but you just don't cut it."

4. If appropriate give a clear and logical explanation as to why you are rejecting or refusing them or their offer.

5. Conclude with an appropriate hope or wish.

— "We wish you the best of luck," for example.

Practice B:

You have just received an official invitation to become the honorary citizen of the month at your local 4-H Club based on your recent hefty donation to their "REACH (Reading and Education for All Children) Fund Drive." You would rather remain anonymous, and you know that accepting their reward will give you attention that you would rather not have. Draft a letter to refuse their request.

REMINDING OR DEMANDING

When you have the unpleasant task of demanding something from somebody, the main rule is that your message must match the nature of the problem. If it is the first time you have to send this type of message to someone, start with a polite reminder. They probably don't deserve a demand just yet.

For the first reminder:

- Be polite and courteous.

- Stress the importance or value of the topic.

- Offer the person a way out—an opportunity to explain their situation and to rectify it without penalty.

For the second reminder:

- Be professional, but less friendly.

- Begin with a reminder of the obligation.

- Ask if there is some extenuating circumstance that is keeping them from their obligation.

- Give a specific deadline for action.

For the third reminder:

- Demand action.

- Disclose consequences of task left undone.

CHAPTER SUMMARY

- When conveying a negative or unpleasant message it is possible to be effective, professional and graceful.

- Being respectful and sincere when your purpose is correcting, adjusting, rejecting, refusing, or demanding can make it easier on you and the recipient of your unpleasant message.

Skill Building

People often make a big deal when they refuse, reject, complain, or demand in their day-to-day conversations. Pay extra attention over the next 24 hours and notice the techniques that people use to get the response they desire. After reading this chapter, can you identify any of the techniques you hear? List some good things people do that aren't in this chapter. Jot down a few things that people do incorrectly, and make a personal note that addresses their mistakes.

Possible Answers to Practice Exercises

Practice A:

I am sending this fax to let you know that I did not receive the additional cable box I ordered last week, despite the appointment I had with your installers today, Saturday the 25th of November. My service-order confirmation number is 36795E.

Unfortunately, I waited at my home at 610 Sixth Street for six hours today and no installation team showed up. I had cancelled plans for the day to make sure I was home and what really upset me was the fact that I didn't even get a call to let me know they weren't coming. I am deeply disturbed by what I feel is a total lack of professionalism. You should know that I have been a customer of the Cable Company for 12 years and have never been late on a payment.

Please consider the fact that I am a valuable, long-time customer and give me the courtesy of a call and an explanation as soon as you are in on Monday. Someone will be home all day Monday, so if possible, send a crew here then.

Practice B:

Thank you for your recent offer to induct me into the 4-H Citizen's Hall of Fame as a *Citizen of the Month* for October. As you know, I have been involved in the REACH program for over 12 years and truly feel it is one of the best community outreach programs available. No, as a matter of fact, *it is the best community program for children in the area!* That is why I have supported this program, and will continue to support it for years to come. However, I must decline this honor. There are several personal reasons why I cannot accept this award. Please be assured that in declining this award I am in no way disassociating myself with the REACH program or with 4-H. As I have said, I will continue to support your outstanding programs for years to come.

Best of luck with the current fund drive!

CHAPTER | 8

TIPS FOR EFFECTIVE REPORTS, REVIEWS, AND INSTRUCTIONS

LEARNING OBJECTIVES

After reading this chapter you should be able to say what you mean when you:

- have to deliver an objective report, or a subjective review
- offer instructions, give directions, or communicate a procedure
- need to convince someone or sell something

PRACTICAL TIPS FOR SPECIALIZED MESSAGES

Employees are often called upon to send a message that has a specialized purpose. A few of the most common special-purpose messages include:

- reports
- reviews

- explanations, instructions, or directions
- persuasive arguments or sales pitches

Reporting

Sometimes your purpose for sending a message to someone is to report on something you saw, did, heard, or studied. When you are reporting, you are actually the eyes and ears for whoever gets your report. It is your responsibility to do it right. Whatever type of reporting you are doing, it will serve your purpose well if your message is accurate, thorough, observant, and objective.

Be Accurate

The most important element of any type of reporting is *accuracy*. In order to ensure accuracy in your reporting:

- Get your facts straight.
- Write everything down; do not rely on your memory.
- Check facts—make sure that:
  - there are no spelling mistakes
  - all dates, times, and numbers are correct
- Verify other data—any facts that you may be unsure of should be checked and double-checked.

Be Thorough

In any report, there are specific items you must cover. These include the five w's—who, what, when, where, and why—and how. This information is basic and should be included in any report. The more specific you can be, the better your chances to effectively communicate the topic you are reporting on.

Reports should always answer the following questions:

- Who was involved?
- What took place?
- When did it happen?
- Where did it happen?
- Why did it take place?
- How did it proceed?

Be Observant

When reporting you have to act like a seasoned reporter and observe the details. Including or not including the details can make or break your report. In business that means it can make all the difference in how or how much you, your company, and/or your co-workers benefit from your report.

The following is a short list of categories that can help you look for specific details when you are compiling data for a report:

time	name	color
location	brand	shape
manner	size	material
tone	type or kind	sound
style	amount	pattern

Be Objective

Keep your impressions and opinions out of the report unless you were specifically instructed to include them, in which case make sure you clearly identify what part of the report contains the objective reporting and what part includes your subjective opinions.

If you have been asked to include a conclusion or your personal recommendations, make sure that this section is logical. Your audience should be able to clearly draw connections between what your conclusion or recommendation says and the facts that you laid out. In order for your subjective review to be valid it must be based upon the objective material presented in the report.

Reviewing

Whether you are reviewing an employee's performance, a new job site, a potential training program, or a new product line, you are communicating important subjective information. Unlike a report, where you must remain objective and present only the facts, a review or appraisal needs your *personal opinion, impression,* or *reaction* to be useful.

In order to say what you mean in a review, make sure you back up your opinions with as much evidence as possible. What distinguishes a good review from a bad review is the support: how much and what kind of evidence is included.

In general, a review should follow this model:

1. Make a strong, clear assertion about the person, place, or thing being reviewed.
2. Offer a brief explanation of why an issue is being reviewed, if applicable.
3. Offer strong evidence supporting the opening assertion.

Try to avoid entirely one-sided reviews (either positive or negative) because they may not be taken as seriously as one that shows a little more balance. Even if your goal is to write a positive review about someone or something, include some details about the bad points so your audience will give you more credibility. Likewise, if you wish to write a negative review, include a few good qualities to show that your opinion is based on looking at the good and the bad.

Practice A:

1. On a separate sheet of paper write a one-paragraph report on what you are doing right now. Assume you are reporting this to a friend who is interested in what your are doing. Hint: Use the five w's.
2. Now add a review paragraph and take a stance regarding the effectiveness of this book or lesson.

Offering Procedures, Instructions, or Directions

At work or at home the more you know, the more you will be asked to explain how to do things. Whether you have to explain procedures or instructions, or give directions to somebody at work or at home, you can be clear and effective by following these tips:

1. Tailor your message to the specific needs of your audience

- Ask yourself the following key questions:

    — Who will be listening to/reading these instructions?

    — What do they need to know? Why?

    — At what level of technicality or familiarity should I be communicating to them?

- If your audience is more than one person, determine a lowest common denominator of knowledge.

    Example: If every member knows A, most know B, and some know C, then you must communicate to level A first. It is O.K. to include basic knowledge, because those who don't need the basics will skip those portions. You just can't omit what someone may not know.

2. Use an introduction to set the stage

- For simple instructions, the introduction can be the title "How to restart your computer in four easy steps."

- For more complicated instructions or procedures, you should tell your audience why they need your instructions. You might choose to include any materials that may be necessary and how long the procedure should take. You may even want to explain what the finished product should look like.

3. Make instructions easy to follow

- Use signposts to let your audience know that they're doing things right such as "if you reach the elevators you have gone too far down the hall."

- Use lists and bullets: Follow chronological order if possible.

- Be as specific as possible: use names, numbers, times, sizes, etc.

- Help your audience by providing warnings:

    Example: "Warning: If the disk is still in the drive make sure you remove it before restarting your computer."

4. Conclude by letting your audience know:

- who to call if they have a problem

- what to expect next or from the results

- how to follow up if necessary, on the procedure.

Other helpful hints for giving instructions or procedures or offering directions include:

- Always make sure you thoroughly understand the procedure yourself, before you attempt to teach others about it.

- Get feedback. Getting feedback is the best way to ensure that your message does what it is supposed to do.

- Before you hand over instructions to someone else, follow them yourself. Don't do what you know how to do, do only what is written, exactly how you have written it. Then ask yourself:

    — Does it work?

    — Are these instructions clear? Complete? Easy to follow?

    — Can they be improved in any way?

Practice B:

On a separate sheet of paper, write directions from your house to the closest post office for your friend from out of town, who will be driving there tomorrow while you are at work.

Convincing or Selling

If you are like most employees, much of your communications at work are aimed at convincing others to think or act in a certain way. If the purpose of your message is to convince or sell an idea, then the following tips will help you say what you mean.

Begin by brainstorming

- Follow the S.A.P. Query Exercise (explained in chapter 5) to ensure you have a clear focus on your:

  1. Audience: Who are you trying to convince?

  2. Purpose: What are you trying to convince them of?

- Compile a list of benefits:

  — You will need to show how your audience will benefit from doing what you are asking. While you may not use the entire list, it is good to have a reserve to look back on if you need to later.

- Gather supporting evidence:

  — You will need to convince your audience that the benefits you promise are real. Specific information regarding who, what, when, and how these benefits have been realized before will help you sell your idea.

- Anticipate objections:

  — You should count on people having objections or reservations about your idea. If you address these concerns using specific examples from your supporting evidence, you will gain credibility and be more convincing.

Follow this general format when you have to convince or sell

1. Catch their attention: Open with a creative introduction.

   - You can tell a story that highlights the eventual benefits that you will discuss.

   - You can tell a story that highlights the pain or missed opportunity that they will experience if they don't buy or act on your idea.

2. State your purpose and link it to potential benefits.

   - Just saying that you wish for someone to do something or to believe something is not enough; you should include the *why* in the purpose statement.

Example: The purpose of this memo is to convince you to participate in the MS Walkathon, either as a sponsor or a walker, because you will not only feel good about the cause, but you will help show the community that our company cares.

3. Summarize the current condition or situation that must change.

- It is always good to remind your audience where they are now, so that they can clearly see the difference that your idea, product, or service will make. How will they know how good it will be if you don't remind them of what they are missing if they don't do or accept your idea?

4. Show the benefits and provide specific evidence.

5. Request a clear and specific action.

CHAPTER SUMMARY

- When you have to deliver a report, you will be effective if you are accurate, thorough, observant, and objective.

- A review should offer your subjective opinion and then back it up with as much evidence as possible.

- Procedures, instructions, and directions need to be easy to follow and should offer contact information in case your audience needs more help.

- When the intent of your message is to sell or convince, the key is to do your homework, so you can convey the personal benefits that your audience will receive from your idea, product, or service, and back them up with specific evidence or examples.

Skill Building

If you are like most people, your mailbox is often full of unwanted solicitations, asking you to donate to this or that cause or to buy this or that new improved product. Since almost all of these letters are uninvited (you didn't ask to receive them) they must grab you and show you benefits quickly or you will file them in the circular filing cabinet under your desk before you even open their envelope. Choose a few of these letters and note how they try to convince you. Do they grab your attention? Clearly describe personal benefits you can expect to enjoy? How do they address your concerns or objections? What action do they ask you to take? Are they effective?

Possible Answers to Practice A:

Francis Baldwin's Seven O'Clock Study Skills Session

This evening is no different than any other evening for young Francis Baldwin, who finishes dinner promptly at 6:55 every night so he can situate himself at his desk, by the big bay window facing east and overlooking Crosby Park, for his nightly half-hour study session. For over a year Francis has been holding these study sessions because he hopes to move into management by his third year and his boss suggested several (eight) books to help him build the skills that are needed to become a good manager. For the past two weeks Francis has been reading about effective communications and teamwork and sharpening his thinking, writing, and conversational skills. Tonight, the twenty-seventh of October, 1998, he is reading about specialized messages and practicing how to construct reports and reviews. As usual, he will read for approximately 10–15 minutes and do exercises for the other 10–15 minutes.

Apparently the study skills sessions are paying off for Francis, who feels better prepared to handle most crises and can talk much more intelligently with his boss since the sessions began. While he admits that there are usually many other things he would rather be doing in the evenings, including playing soccer on Mondays and bowling on Thursdays, he considers the sessions an investment that will pay off for him in a big way over the years. He feels that, while young (20), he should do everything he can to put himself in a position to succeed, and judging by his reporting and reviewing skills, he is well on his way to success.

Possible Answers to Practice B:

Answers will vary but make sure your directions are as specific as possible and include signposts and warnings if necessary. Did you include the number for the post office in case your friend gets lost?

Directions to Post Office (233-3333)

Proceed down Fifth street a half block to the park. Make a right on Park Avenue (it's one way and you can't go anywhere else). Proceed four blocks south (past the light at Seventh Street) and make a right on Ninth Street at the light. Go west on Ninth Street past three lights (three long blocks) and the post office is on your right about halfway down the block after the third light, between Fifth and Fourth Avenue. You can park either directly in front of the building, or go to the next light at Fourth Avenue and make a right and then another right on the next block at Eighth Street where you will see the back of the building on your right halfway down the block. There is a big parking lot in the back.

CHAPTER | 9

BUILDING BETTER LISTENING SKILLS

LEARNING OBJECTIVES

After reading this chapter you should be able to communicate more effectively by utilizing active listening skills to:

- build a more positive relationship with the speaker
- involve more of your brainpower when listening
- avoid distractions and maintain a keen focus on the speaker

HEARING VS. LISTENING

hear: *to perceive sounds with the ear*

listen: *the process of receiving, constructing meaning from, and responding to spoken and/or nonverbal messages*

There is a big difference between hearing and listening. Everyone with capable ears can hear. It is an automatic process, you don't even have to think about it. Listening, on the other hand, requires a decision on your part to actively engage in a task that requires *skill, concentration,* and *mental sharpness.*

The end result of effective listening is understanding and feedback. When you successfully listen to someone and actively pursue meaning and understanding, you will go through a process that includes analyzing and evaluating the incoming message, understanding the message and its implications, and responding appropriately with feedback and a message of your own.

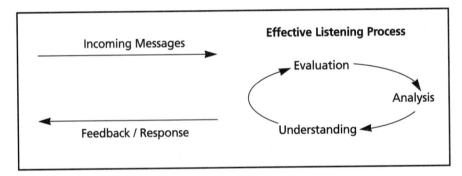

Practice:

Read the following examples. A very basic message is being sent. Answer the questions accordingly.

1. It is 12:15 and your colleagues walk by your cubicle saying, "We're going out to lunch."

   What do you hear?

   What do you understand?

2. You're sitting at your desk organizing your inbox messages and your boss comments as she walks by, "Cal has set four appointments already; how many calls have you made this morning?"

   What do you hear?

   What do you understand?

3. You're alone in your office with one other employee and you hear him say very loudly, "I wish I knew how to fix the printer."

What do you hear?

What do you understand?

Answers:

1. Heard: "We're going out to lunch."

   Understood: I have been invited to join my friends for lunch.

2. Heard: "Cal has set four appointments already; how many calls have you made this morning?"

   Understood: My boss feels that I should be on the phone making appointments, not organizing my desk.

3. Heard: "I wish I knew how to fix the printer."

   Understood: My colleague wants me to help him with his printer problem.

Tips for Active Listening

In order to understand the incoming message, you must first analyze and evaluate its meaning and implications. To do this you must listen actively to the speaker. The following tips should help you become a better, active listener.

1. Create a positive and energetic relationship with the sender

Since you already know that communication is a two-way process, with both the sender and receiver actively engaged in processing messages, it should be no surprise that listening works the same way. Because listening is a two-way process, and involves feedback and questioning, it is important that you develop a positive and energetic relationship with the speaker or sender. As in any physical exercise, if your energy level is up, your performance will be better—the same is true with listening. If you are half-asleep, you can't listen effectively and you surely won't be establishing a good rapport with the sender.

In order to create a positive and energetic relationship with the sender, especially when you are engaged in a face-to-face meeting, follow these tips:

- Give the speaker your undivided attention
    - maintain eye contact
    - keep a positive posture
    - don't lean back in your chair
    - don't fidget
    - don't prop your head up with your hands
    - don't rest your head on your desk
    - don't chew your pen or obviously chew gum
    - don't eat (if you must, ask permission first)
- Participate through non-verbal feedback
    - nod your head
    - lean forward
    - make appropriate gestures
    - smile
- Participate with verbal feedback
    - use verbal affirmations

    For example: 'yes,' 'uh huh,' 'I understand,' 'really,' 'wow,' 'is that so,' etc.

    - ask questions
    - paraphrase aloud. For example:
- 'So what you are saying is' . . .
- 'If I understand you correctly' . . .
- 'In summary, you are saying' . . .
    - encourage additional supporting facts
    - ask for clarifications and examples when applicable

— reflect the implications. For example:

- 'So if what you are saying is true, would that mean' . . .
- 'Are you implying that' . . .
- 'Would that apply to' . . .

  — give examples when appropriate

- Be professional

  — tolerate any bad habits or techniques the speaker may have

  — judge message and content, not the personal traits of the sender

  — avoid generalizations you might be inclined to make about the speaker

  — control your own emotions

  — be objective

  — hold off judgment of the message until all the information is presented

  — do not criticize the delivery or the technique of the presenter

2. Actively utilize your capacity to think faster than the sender can speak

The human brain is capable of processing much more information than the input of one speaker. Have you ever heard of the secretary that can talk on the phone, type a letter, listen to their boss yelling instructions from the other room, and listen to the news on the radio, all at the same time? While this is probably a gross exaggeration of the multi-tasking possibilities of the human brain, it does at least highlight a good point: you are capable of much more than hearing what someone is saying when they speak to you.

In order to utilize more of your brainpower when in a listening situation, follow these tips:

- Be observant

  — take notes

  — summarize what was said

  — look for opportunities to learn new ideas

- Analyze and evaluate the data

  — identify and concentrate on the main idea

  — connect the supporting details to the main idea

  — challenge the argument in your own mind

- Internalize the message

  — connect new information to your own experiences

  — ask yourself, 'What implications does this message have?'

  — think of how you can use this information personally and professionally

  — listen for nonverbal cues, changes in tone, delivery, or pace and write down suggestions as to what those changes may mean to the content

3. Avoid distractions

Distractions come in many forms and are the most common barriers to effective listening. Follow these tips to avoid distractions:

- Don't

  — daydream

  — watch the clock

  — plan other activities

  — focus on the bad habits of the speaker

  — criticize the speaker's accent, clothing, hair, etc. . . .

  — do your nails

  — fiddle with objects

CHAPTER SUMMARY

- Listening—the process of receiving, constructing meaning from, and responding to spoken and/or nonverbal messages—requires understanding, analysis, and evaluation, not just hearing.

- Active listening techniques can help you get more out of the communication process by building a better relationship between you and the speaker, utilizing your capacity to think faster than the speaker can talk and by helping you avoid distractions.

Skill Building

Make a photocopy of the "Tips for Active Listening" and tuck it into a notepad. Refer to it the next time you have a meeting or must listen to a speaker—just make sure you refer to the list before the meeting or lecture, during breaks, and immediately after, not during. Take notes as to which tips were difficult to follow and which ones were easy to use.

CHAPTER | 10

PARTICIPATING SUCCESSFULLY IN MEETINGS

LEARNING OBJECTIVES

After reading this chapter you should be able to:

- plan a successful meeting and draft a detailed agenda
- actively participate in a meeting
- follow up with your colleagues after a meeting to ensure success

HIGH-POWERED COMMUNICATIONS PLATFORM

Meetings represent a very high-powered form of communication, because they stress oral communications and include multiple participants. While there are countless specific purposes for having a meeting, usually the general purpose is to make a decision or collaborate on a project. Think about it: If your goal is merely to inform a group of people, couldn't you just send them all a memo?

Meetings also provide a great forum for sharing information and feedback among a group of people in "real time." If you need instant feedback on ideas and you want everyone to benefit from discussing multiple options based on different perspectives, then a meeting is the best way to do it.

In order to be effective, meetings must be planned ahead of time, follow an agenda, and be followed up afterwards to make sure that all action items were taken care of. The rest of this chapter will provide you with a helpful guide for planning, running, and following up your meetings.

PRE-MEETING PLANNING

The most important tool for running a successful meeting is pre-meeting planning. An efficient, productive meeting will follow only in the wake of a well-developed meeting plan. The key elements to pre-meeting planning include:

1. objectives and outcomes
2. participant selection and background information
3. detailed agenda
4. logistics

1. Objectives and Outcomes

The leader or facilitator of the meeting should set very explicit goals and clearly communicate what the purpose of the meeting is to all participants. The more focused the goals, the easier it will be to achieve them. The most effective way to set goals for a meeting includes the use of objectives and desired outcomes. The objectives state the goal in a meaningful and concrete way, while the outcomes tie the objectives to particular events that should occur during or after the meeting.

An ineffective purpose would be "to increase the effectiveness of the marketing department." While this may be a good general goal for the company, it is not detailed enough to provide the necessary direction for a group of people in a meeting. A better stated goal would take the form of objectives and outcomes:

The objective of today's meeting will be to weigh the benefits and challenges of each PC upgrade proposal and to determine the one that best fits the marketing department's long-term goals and budget. At the completion of the meeting, we will select a plan (by vote) and elect a committee of five members to implement the selected plan. Those members will then draft an outline of an implementation timeline.

2. Participant Selection and Background Information

In order to include only individuals who are relevant to the meeting's purpose, ask yourself the following questions:

- Who will be responsible for achieving our objectives?
- Who will be most affected by any decisions made in the meeting?
- Who can best make the decisions?

Those members that can contribute the most should be included in the meeting, while members that are only affected slightly or are not actively involved in the decision-making process should not be there.

Once you know who will best serve the purpose of the meeting, it is important that they receive all important information ahead of time. Spending needless time during the meeting while everybody reads a 12-page report is not a good use of time.

In our meeting example from earlier, the following data would have been included with the Objectives and Outcomes memo:

- copies of proposals from three outside vendors for the PC project
- a summary of a needs analysis conducted by a training consultant
- an internal report generated by the IS department that includes facts and figures regarding projected costs for implementation and support of the project

3. Detailed Agenda

A detailed agenda is a tool for achieving your goals in a meeting. An agenda is a list of topics or main ideas to be discussed in the meeting. It is more than a recipe for a successful meeting; it is the how-to guide. The agenda will show participants, in advance, exactly what topics will be covered in the meeting, allowing them to prepare their input ahead of time and think about how they can actively contribute to the meeting. Of course the agenda will also be used during the meeting as a guide to keep the discussion on track and to make sure all the key topics are covered. The agenda provides order and logic to the meeting, and greatly increases the chances of achieving the objectives and outcomes.

In our continuing example, the agenda would look something like this:

1:00 Opening: Irma Selig, VP of Marketing

- Review of Objectives and Outcomes
- Current status of marketing department
- Future direction of the department

1:30 Report from Edward Thomas, VP of Marketing Services

- Updated cost analysis of proposed PC project

1:45 Report/Discussion form Jan Kilner, VP of Organizational Development

- Review of Needs Analysis
- Recommendations/Discussion

2:30 PC Project Vote, Facilitated by Don Evers

- Benefits and challenges of different proposed plans
- Vote on project
- Vote on new members for implementation team

3:45 New Implementation Team Meeting (others dismissed)

- Draft outline for project
- Draft timeline for project
- Set up benchmarks and future meeting dates

4. Logistics

Logistics planning may be the easiest part of pre-meeting planning, yet it is often overlooked. Logistics planning refers to the arrangement of key resources including the time, place, equipment, and setting. Planning the logistics helps to improve the effectiveness of the meeting for two reasons: 1) there may be physical considerations that have to be met in order to achieve the objectives and cover the agenda, and 2) there may be affective considerations that have to be met in order for the meeting's participants to be productive.

Physical considerations include the need for specific equipment or facilities requirements such as a computer with a wall projector, a VCR player, a teleconferencing phone, or wheelchair access. If anything physical is needed for the meeting, it should be arranged beforehand.

Affective considerations include anything that will affect the attitudes, feelings, or emotions of the participants. For instance, if the meeting will require much dialogue then the seating should allow for everyone to have eye contact with everyone else. If the meeting will include brainstorming (a very creative process) it should not take place immediately after lunch when most participants will be digesting and far from their creative peak.

Practice:

1. What is wrong with the following memo?

2. How would you make it better, based on the guidelines in this chapter for a planning a meeting?

MEMO

TO: **All Employees**
FROM: **Alfred E. Neuman, Chairperson—Executive Committee**
RE: **Benefits Meeting**

The executive committee invites all employees to join us in the executive conference suite this Friday for a very important meeting to discuss our health benefits plan. Coffee and doughnuts will be served.

ACTIVE PARTICIPATION DURING THE MEETING

While planning can make all the difference in the world regarding the effectiveness of a meeting, the real test comes during the actual meeting, when virtually anything can happen. In order to make the most of your pre-meeting planning and to effectively communicate with all parties involved during a meeting, you should follow these tips:

- respect everyone's time
- preview and review the objectives
- follow the agenda
- encourage active participation

RESPECT EVERYONE'S TIME

Meetings should always start on time, because, as noted in earlier chapters, time is money, and attendees that are punctual should not have their time wasted. Not only does punctuality show respect for every meeting attendee, it also sends a signal to latecomers that tardiness will not be tolerated. Unless a keynote speaker is running late, or the highest-ranking member is late, all meetings should start on time. Some weekly or monthly meetings utilize a closed-door policy for latecomers: If you are more than two minutes late, you are not allowed to enter the meeting at all. This sends a very strong message to all attendees regarding respect for each other's time.

It is also a good idea to appoint a timekeeper to make sure things move along quick enough to cover the complete agenda in the allotted time. Meetings that do not end on time can be disastrous because participants lose focus and may have to leave before the conclusion of the meeting. *It is better to have less on the agenda and finish the meeting in the allotted time, than to include more topics than there is time for.*

PREVIEW AND REVIEW THE OBJECTIVES

Starting the meeting off by previewing the objectives and outcomes gets everyone focused on the same goal. Even when the agenda is given out ahead of time, and every member is familiar with the objectives and outcomes, it is important to take a few minutes at the start of the meeting to discuss the goals. This puts everybody "on the same page" and clears up any ambiguity members might have about why they are at the meeting.

If the meeting seems to be going off track it is always good to review the objectives and bring the discussion back to the heart of the matter. Often, towards the end of meetings, when everybody is "warmed up" and the creative juices are flowing, interesting discussions can go on and on without really adding value to the meeting. To avoid this it is always good to list the intended outcomes on the published agenda, so there is a visible target and everyone can see whether the discussion is on target or not.

In our example, the agenda includes action items that are part of the objectives and outcomes. These items include a vote as well as the formulation of a new subcommittee to run the proposed project. As the meeting progresses, it is clear to everyone why they are debating PC issues—they know they will have to vote and may sit on a committee to enact the plan—and this helps them be more attentive throughout.

FOLLOW THE AGENDA

In order to progress effectively toward the intended objectives and outcomes of the meeting, it is tantamount to follow the published agenda. In more formal meetings, do not discuss topics that are not included on the agenda. On the other hand, in informal meetings, topics that may be relevant to the discussion but not on the agenda can be discussed. If the meeting is formal it may follow formal procedures, but if the meeting is informal, there may not be any agreed-upon procedure for having a productive discussion.

In any case, the key to following the agenda is to frequently ask the question: "Will the item we are currently discussing help us meet our objectives in this meeting?" If the answer is a definite 'Yes' then you are following your agenda. If the answer is a 'Maybe' then you need to clarify and summarize how the current discussion will help the published objectives be met. If the answer is a 'No' then the discussion should be dropped and the focus should be shifted back to the agenda.

ENCOURAGE ACTIVE PARTICIPATION

The very essence of a meeting is the ability to discuss important matters with attendees who may have different insights and valuable input. Therefore, it is important that *all members in the meeting actively participate*. You can use the following techniques to encourage everyone's participation, whether or not you are the meeting chairperson:

Encourage the Free Flow of Pertinent Ideas from Everybody

Effective meetings are more than just a leader, or a guest speaker "showing their stuff." As a member focused on the meeting's objectives, it is your duty to encourage and offer ideas that are pertinent to the discussion. By offering your input and asking others to join the discussion, you are being an effective participant and encouraging active participation.

Use Active Listening Skills

You will be doing more listening than talking in meetings, so stay sharp by following the tips listed in chapter 9. They work especially well in meetings.

Utilize Every Mind

It is a good idea to ask the opinions of varied people throughout the meeting. If the same people seem to be dominating the discussion, make a point to ask the opinion of someone else. By involving as many people as possible you are adding to the richness of the knowledge pool.

Reward Active Participation

Most individuals like to be given credit when credit is due, so reward good ideas by giving credit to those who make them. By giving due credit to those participants who are active, you are encouraging continued participation.

POST-MEETING FOLLOW UP

Several action items should be performed after a meeting to ensure that the objectives and outcomes are achieved. These items include:

Summarize the Objectives and Outcomes

At the completion of a meeting, a summary of the objectives that were met should be read in order to make sure that all of the participants understand what was accomplished in relation to what was intended.

A Call to Action

All participants should know what, if any, individual tasks they are responsible for completing and when they are expected to complete them.

Written Summary

Published minutes from the meeting or a written summary should be distributed to all participants of the meeting. This memo should include a detailed version of the tasks and timelines agreed upon at the end of the meeting.

CHAPTER SUMMARY

- Meetings are an important part of work and life and represent a very rich communications forum where multiple viewpoints and excited debate can lead to important decisions.

- Successful meetings are planned in advance and include a detailed agenda with objectives and intended outcomes.

- Meetings are more successful if they proceed in a timely manner, cover the written agenda, and involve as many participants as possible

- Summarizing the results and giving members clear follow-up tasks helps ensure that the intended outcomes are achieved.

Possible Answers to Practice Exercises

1. First, the objective as it is written in the memo is too vague to serve any real purpose. Merely discussing health care benefits is neither concrete nor actionable and there is no intended outcome. What will happen to signify that the meeting accomplished its goal?

   Second, the audience is too general. If the entire employee population actually showed up for the meeting, could it possibly be effective?

   Third, there is no information relevant to the meeting included or referenced, nor is there a detailed agenda. How do I know specifically what will be covered so I can prepare my comments for the meeting?

   Finally, the logistics are all wrong. Do we know what time the meeting is taking place? Could the executive conference suite (which seats 25 people at most) hold all 1,248 employees? Even if only 5% of the employee population attend the meeting, half of them would be sitting on the window sills, crammed into doorways, or lining the hallways near the suite just to get a glimpse of the discussion. Would this be a fire code violation?

2. First, including a meaningful and concrete objective and an actionable outcome would be more effective. The objective could be stated, "to qualify the applicant pool of health benefit providers by reviewing and debating the merits of each company's proposed benefits package,"

while the outcome could be, " . . . to choose a provider whose services best match the company's mission and the employees needs."

Second, if the executive committee really wanted to get every employee's opinion and suggestion regarding the new health benefits provider, they should have utilized different formats for their communications. For example, if they felt face-to-face meetings were important, they could hold meetings with key department supervisors and these supervisors could then hold their own meetings with their managers who could in turn meet with every one of their employees to get feedback. Information collected from the employees could be documented and sent back up the chain of command to the supervisors, who could then present the ideas back to the executive committee.

Third, an agenda that reflects the goals in the objectives and outcomes statements could be drafted and given to the supervisors and the managers, and even distributed to employees via the company's internal web site. The proposals that will be voted on and any supporting materials (such as statistics compiled by the human resources department and the current health benefits provider, as well as pertinent data collected from outside consultants or from the Internet), should be sent to the supervisors and managers or made available on the company's internal web site.

Finally, if the executive committee felt that the entire company should see the discussion and the ensuing vote, then they could tape the proceedings or simulcast them over closed circuit TV or via the internal web site.

CHAPTER | 11

OVERCOMING COMMON BARRIERS TO VERBAL COMMUNICATIONS

LEARNING OBJECTIVES

After reading this chapter you should be able to overcome the most common barriers to effective verbal communications.

WHAT WENT WRONG?

Despite your best efforts to communicate effectively, there will be many times that your messages won't be received as intended. There will be times when messages never make it to the recipient ("the dog ate my homework") and times when they make it but are illegible, inaccurate, or erroneously decoded ("I said four tickets for the second game, not two tickets for the fourth game").

Communication barriers can be grouped into verbal and non-verbal. Sometimes it is what you say that causes a problem in the communication process, other times it is how you say it that causes the problem. This chapter will provide you with tips for overcoming common barriers to verbal communications—what you say, while the next chapter will focus on overcoming non-verbal communications barriers—how you say it.

VERBAL COMMUNICATION BARRIERS

Verbal barriers to communication are caused by mistakes in the message (such as improper word choices) or by errors on the receiver's part (such as misunderstandings). Often problems occur in communications because the symbols (words) chosen to express meaning are not used correctly, translated properly, or completely understood by the receiver.

Many instances of failed communication can be traced to a lack of knowledge or a misuse of words on the part of the sender. In order to avoid miscommunication due to these potential barriers, utilize the tips in this chapter.

Category: Lack of Knowledge

Barrier: Lack of proper understanding in the subject area of your message

Solution:

- read trade journals or professional magazines pertaining to the subject matter
- borrow a book from the library
- buy a book from a major bookstore
- attend a seminar
- spend time searching the Internet for material on the subject matter

Barrier: Lack of knowledge of the audience (the receiver)

Solution:

- investigate her perspective
- ask questions of him
- ask questions of her peers

- identify what factors will affect his perception of the topic and anticipate how you should frame your message accordingly

- if you are unable to understand his perspective, at least appreciate how it differs from yours and consider that difference when you construct your message

Category: Misuse or Misunderstanding in Language

Barrier: Interpretation errors when translating between two different languages in an oral discussion

Solution:

- Use a translator that you know and trust.

    — If you are the sender and have to use the receiver's translator, you can never be sure that she is translating accurately. Therefore, it is better if you know your translator.

Barrier: Translation errors when translating between two different languages in a written document

Solution:

- Translate into the second language and then translate the text back into your own language, using a different translator. This will ensure that the translation did not distort or lose your meaning.

Barrier: Ambiguous meanings or directions

Solution:

- Be as specific as possible when making observations and giving directions.

- Include signposts in directions: For example, which directions would you rather follow?

    Take route 22 west to Oaktree Road.

    or

From Teaton, go two miles west on Route 22. Just past the Amoco station on the right you will see a very large oak tree with a fruit stand underneath. Make a right at the next intersection (approximately 30 feet from the fruit stand) on Oaktree Road.

- Use concrete words instead of abstract words whenever possible.

— Here are some examples:

Abstract Language	Concrete Language
business communication . . .	letter, fax, memo, etc.
transportation . . .	bus, car, train, plane, etc.
tools . . .	scissors, computers, software, etc.
few, several, some . . .	two, three, four, etc. . . .
many, a lot, a bunch . . .	sixteen, twenty-five, etc.
sometimes . . .	every 2 months, etc.
often, always . . .	every 2 minutes, every day, etc.
most . . .	98%, 4 out of 5, etc.
far . . .	200 miles, three months, etc.

Practice A: List 10 abstract words that you frequently use and then list at least two concrete words that would clear up any ambiguity.

Abstract Word   **Concrete Replacements**

1. _____   _____

2. _____   _____

3. _____   _____

4. _____   _____

5. _____   _____

6. _____   _____

7. _____   _____

8. _____   _____

9. _____   _____

10. _____   _____

Barrier: Semantics—most words can mean different things to different people at different times.

Solution:

- Since many words have multiple meanings and can be interpreted differently—even in the same or similar situations—choose words that mean exactly what you are trying to express.

  — The more possible common interpretations a word has, the greater the chance it may be misinterpreted. For example, if the words broad, player, hump, cut, kill, juice, or jam were used in a business setting, would you know how to interpret them? Could you replace these words with ones that would more clearly deliver your intended message?

- Consider the connotation of key words, especially in conjunction with your understanding of the intended receiver.

  — Many words are very emotionally charged and can distort your message or even deliver an unintended message. Some examples include gay, boss, love, bad, right, wrong, truth, lie, false.

Practice B: List your reactions to the words included as examples in the above section on semantics. Do you think everyone has the same reaction as you to these words?

Barrier: Inappropriate use of expressions—phrases often have entirely different meanings than their literal interpretation.

Solution:

- Use expressions with extreme caution, making sure that they are appropriate.
- Use expressions sparingly.

  — Constant use of expressions will not only dilute your ability to communicate effectively, it will cheapen your reputation as a good communicator and cause even further miscommunication.

- Avoid clichés, overused expressions that have become trite (*the early bird catches the worm*).

Barrier: Inappropriate use of jargon

Definition: Jargon is a highly technical vocabulary used within a specialized group of professionals to communicate efficiently with each other. It is non-sensical or incoherent to those outside the group. For example, your doctor takes his stethoscope to your chest and speaks into his handheld recorder, "CV shows RRR, S1S2 without murmurs, rubs or gallups." You don't know what this means, yet to his colleagues this makes perfect sense. However, it becomes clear when he turns to you and says, "everything sounds fine."

Solution:

- Limit the use of jargon to those within your professional group

- Avoid using jargon with people unfamiliar with it

- Avoid using jargon to impress others

Barrier: Inappropriate use of slang

Definition: Slang is similar to jargon in that it is a vocabulary used by sub-groups. Slang, however, is informal and temporary. Slang often uses common words and twists the meaning and the connotation to add significance when used within the group. For example, if a teen called you "phat" you shouldn't take offense or go on a diet based on this comment. This is a compliment: it either means you have a stylish look or did something that was considered "cool."

Solution:

- Limit slang usage to informal face-to-face communications

- Avoid using slang in a professional setting

Barrier: Inappropriate use of euphemisms

Definition: Euphemisms are positive or neutral expressions used in place of negative or unpleasant descriptions. For example, how often have you heard *downsizing* used instead of *firing employees* and *passed away* instead of *died*?

Solution:

- Use euphemisms only when they are necessary for politeness

- Avoid using euphemisms to minimize results of an action

- Avoid using euphemisms to purposely leave the listener in the dark or with a only a vague notion of the truth because you think they don't want to hear it

- Avoid using euphemisms to avoid confrontation or criticism—both should be dealt with sooner rather than later if they are a result of your message

CHAPTER SUMMARY

- Knowing the subject of your message and your audience will help you overcome a knowledge barrier to communication.

- Using a trusted translator for bilingual discussion and translating written messages to the intended language and then back into your language will help you avoid translation barriers to communication.

- Choosing your words carefully, being specific when giving directions, and curbing the use of expressions, jargon, slang, and euphemisms will help you overcome the most common language barriers to communication.

Skill Building

Ask a friend of the opposite sex who is employed in a different line of work than you to list his reactions to the example
words from the semantics section and compare their list to
yours. Are your feelings about the words the same? How
could the differences be a barrier to communications between
the two of you?

CHAPTER | 12

OVERCOMING COMMON NON-VERBAL COMMUNICATION BARRIERS

LEARNING OBJECTIVES

After reading this chapter you should be able to:

- overcome common non-verbal barriers to communication, and select the proper channel for your communications

NON-VERBAL COMMUNICATION BARRIERS

How you say something and how someone responds says much about the acceptance and understanding of the message. Often, selecting the wrong format (channel) for your message can cause problems in the communication process, while at other times non-verbal cues or feedback are responsible for misunderstandings.

This chapter will cover these non-verbal barriers to effective communication and provide you with tips to overcome them.

Category: Improper Channel Selection

Barrier: Ambiguity of channel selection

Solution:

- determine ahead of time the method you will be using to deliver your message and construct the message accordingly
- analyze choices before committing to a channel

Follow the diagram below to help you select the proper channel for your message:

IF THIS IS MOST IMPORTANT . . .	. . . USE THIS CHANNEL
• Speed You need to deliver the message right away, and receive feedback as quickly as possible.	• Face-to-face (if you are in the same office) • Email (if you don't think a face-to-face meeting is needed) • Electronic chat session (if you are able) • Video-conference (if the message is very complicated and requires immediate feedback as in face-to-face, but you are not in the same office and can't meet)
• Factual Accuracy The main purpose of your message is to deliver detailed information to the receiver, such as specific instructions, policies, or procedures and you need a permanent copy.	• Any permanent written document such as a — Letter — Memo — Proposal — Email (often with a document attached)
• Feedback Accuracy Your message will be very interactive and you need immediate feedback from the audience (the receiver).	• Face-to-face (if possible) • Video-conference (when necessary and available) • Interactive electronic media — Real-time chat — Web-based collaboration (with chat and/or voice capabilities)

• **Personal and Confidential** The message is of a personal nature and should not be distributed, archived for future reference, or accessible to anyone else.	• Face-to-face • Telephone • Letter • Memo *Note: Depending on the level of trust between you and the receiver and the degree of personal information being exchanged, you should choose the best of the above verbal channels. Ask yourself, "If someone happens to get a peek at this letter or memo, would it jeopardize the status, position, relationship, job, integrity, or reputation of me or the receiver?" *If the answer is yes, then deliver it face-to-face.*
• **Very Important Information** The information you are delivering can be considered extremely important, such a firing somebody, or giving them a raise or performance review.	• Face-to-face • Letter • Memo • Email *Note: Very important messages should be delivered using both oral and written methods of communication. For instance, a performance review would include 1) an email or memo reminding the party of the review, 2) a face-to-face review meeting, and 3) a follow-up letter summing up the review and making recommendations based on the review.

Practice:

Select the proper channel for the following messages.

1. It is 10:30 and you have to confirm a 12:00 meeting for your boss.

2. You need to invite your entire office to a party for the receptionist next week.

3. The bill for the office supplies that just got delivered is wrong (you have 30-day terms with the supplier).

4. You have to warn an employee that one more missed meeting will result in an official reprimand and will jeopardize her bonus.

Answers:

1. First choice is to phone; if you can't get the person, then fax. There are no other options.

2. Email will do unless it is a surprise. Then you may want to hand-deliver invitations or talk to everyone face-to-face about it.

3. Send a letter with a copy of the erroneous invoice.

4. Since it is the warning before an official reprimand, you can use email or a face-to-face meeting. The reprimand will surely be in a formal letter and must warrant a meeting as well.

Barrier: Inconsistent or conflicting signals

Often, without knowing it, you send a non-verbal message to your audience that conflicts with your spoken words or something you have written. For example, you forget an important document to a big meeting with your boss and assure her that it is taken care of and you can get it to her later. She will invariably interpret the non-verbal cue—that you either aren't finished with it, or don't value it as important—no matter what you say or do afterwards. Or you are asked by your friend one more time "You are sure that it's not a problem?" and you answer with an almost inaudible "yes" as you look down at the floor. He will certainly feel that you are not comfortable with the situation and that you are hiding the fact that it may be a problem, due to your lack of eye contact and unsure voice or tone.

Solution:

- Always be aware of your body language—posture and eye positioning are key factors in how the message is delivered

- Make an effort to *practice what you preach* or *preach what you practice*

- Think about your delivery—speech patterns and inflections—and make sure they are in line with your thoughts

Category: Emotional Interference

Excessive emotions, prejudices, and stereotypes can stop effective communication dead in its tracks because neither the sender nor the receiver is thinking logically. This emotional interference can cause a lapse of reason and can cause escalating conflict and even ill-will.

Barrier: Excessive Emotion

When negative emotions are high, especially anger or resentment, and communication does not follow a logical path, effective communication is next to impossible. Often in these cases participants take the messages personally, with the sender attacking the receiver or the receiver feeling like the sender is on the attack and attacking back.

Solution:

- Be aware of emotionally-charged dialogue and avoid escalation by focusing on the content and meaning rather than the emotions

- Use language like 'I feel that' and 'the way I see it' to show the other party that you are expressing opinions or feelings.

For example, if you feel you are being personally attacked by someone in a discussion, instead of attacking back, it's better to stop the situation before it gets worse and say 'That last comment you made makes me feel like I am being attacked personally.' This will give the other person a chance to re-send the message, paying special attention to any emotions.

This usually discharges a heightened emotional environment rather quickly and puts the focus back on content.

Barrier: Stereotyping or Prejudice

Definitions: A stereotype is when you believe that a group of people think, act, or are exactly the same, despite a lack of supporting evidence. As far as communication is concerned, prejudice is having a dislike or like for something or someone that is so strong that you are unable to use reason to listen to or understand ideas from or about them. Prejudices are often caused by stereotypes.

Solution:

- Separate the message from the sender.

- Listen to the message, not the sender.

- Focus on the content and the meaning rather than the delivery or the person.

- Challenge yourself to use reason in your dialogue, not emotion.

- Find the logic in the message and attempt to use similar patterns of logic in your own messages and feedback.

CHAPTER SUMMARY

- By selecting the proper channel or format for your message before you compose it, you will overcome a common barrier to communication.

- By being aware of your body language and sending the right non-verbal messages, you can overcome another common barrier to communication.

- By separating emotions and content, you can communicate more effectively.

Skill Building

Notice how many times you send a letter, make a phone call, or meet with someone tomorrow. Ask yourself, 'Did I use the most effective channel?' If you answer 'no,' then why and what would have been better? Ask yourself if your body language is working with or against your intended message.

PART | III

WORKING EFFECTIVELY IN TEAMS

Individuals behave differently when they work in teams. Teams have a way of bringing the best out of some people, while driving others to exhibit behavior that is perplexing and troubling. In any case, to work effectively as a part of team, you will need to be aware of some of the pitfalls involved with team work, as well as how you can be a successful member or team leader.

Knowing how teams develop and the types of roles members play can certainly help you be a positive influence on any team. Leadership roles within a team require specific traits that you should be aware of, because in order to succeed you will have be a leader within a team at some point or another. In Part III, you will not only learn how to deal with conflict in a team, you will also learn about different models of problem solving within teams. Finally, you will be able to improve your team's performance by using the evaluation and feedback techniques explained in chapter 20.

CHAPTER | 13

STAGES OF TEAM DEVELOPMENT AND TEAM NORMS

LEARNING OBJECTIVES

After reading this chapter you should be able to:

- identify the current stage of development for any team
- identify the norms for any team
- help create positive team norms within your own team

TEAMS GET BETTER WITH AGE

Think of a team that you were once a part of. Can you remember the first meeting? Did things get better after that? In the beginning, tensions were probably high since members were unclear of their roles and weren't comfortable with each other yet. Over time, however, the dynamics of the team changed, and individuals began to get comfortable with each other, until eventually the team grew more productive as members began cooperating and collaborating.

Behavioral psychologists and organizational development specialists basically agree that all teams evolve: the members grow together through distinct stages of development and eventually end up as a productive unit—a cohesive group. Of course some successful teams become far more cohesive than others, while some unsuccessful teams never quite evolve to the point where members work together well.

Many models exist that describe the stages of team development, and while they all use different titles and a different number of stages, they share these common findings:

- The stages represent a progression: both production and cohesiveness increase from beginning to end (although there are times in the middle when tensions run high and productivity and unity drop for a bit).

- There is no absolute time frame for a team to progress through the stages: some teams have deadlines or are in existence for only a day or two and progress within hours, while other teams may take weeks or even months to progress from one stage to another.

- Each stage has its own problems and challenges for the team's leaders and members: leaders and members experience different types of challenges and problems at different stages in their team's existence.

THE LEARNINGEXPRESS MODEL OF TEAM DEVELOPMENT

As all teams develop, they pass through a series of phases, which can be grouped into three stages. Members exhibit common characteristics through each stage. The stages include:

1. forming
2. performing
3. reforming

Stage 1—Forming

Initially, in the beginning of the *Forming Stage*, members see themselves as individuals, not as part of a team. During this orientation phase members may be outwardly polite to each other, but underneath they are anxious because of unfamiliarity with the setting. Some members may even be angered or agitated because of a high level of tension due to a fear of the unknown. Uncertainty abounds and members ask themselves: "Why am I here? What am I going to do? Who should I be? Where do I fit in? What role can I play? Who can I trust? Who do I have to watch closely?" During this phase, team leaders need to be very directive and take charge in order to move the team along and get tasks accomplished.

As members begin to talk to each other and work with each other after the orientation phase, they seek to acquaint themselves with the new environment, while at the same time trying to influence other members and test them to see what behaviors and attitudes will be tolerated. This working in phase is often marked by clashing personal agendas as members begin to get their bearings and assert their roles. Yet even as they assert themselves, many members are still clarifying their own roles, so tensions often run very high and conflict almost always erupts. The working in phase can be very difficult for the team and is, in fact, the most crucial time of development for the team. Teams that get through this phase intact usually succeed, while most teams that fail or break up do so during this phase.

During the working in phase, teams are wrought with disagreements as opinions and attitudes begin to merge and groups organize to take charge. Some members enjoy the power struggles and seek to win over other members just because they can, while others attempt to take control because they feel their knowledge, skills, or experience can help them lead the group. Some members try to focus the group on the tasks at hand, while other members are more focused on working out the personal differences and improving the group's social dynamics. As you can guess, during this period of development most members feel quite dissatisfied and they sense a lack of unity. During this phase of development team leaders need to shift more towards a coaching leadership style, as they facilitate between competing groups and/or individuals to keep the team focused on its goals.

Whether due to natural evolution or with the help of a newly appointed leader, a settling in phase final occurs and this marks the start of Stage 2, *Performing*.

Stage 2—Performing

The settling in phase of a team occurs as members begin to assimilate and resolve their individual differences in order to serve the goals of the team. Self-serving roles are dropped as team-serving roles give rise to acceptance and understanding. Standards for acceptable behavior and attitudes within the group develop, and as they take their hold, cohesion and unity begin to thrive. During this phase of development team leaders should maintain a supportive leadership style, as they continue to support the group in their efforts to reach their goals together.

Once the team is past the settling in phase it enters the production phase of development, where its members focus on performing the tasks at hand to further the group's goals. At this stage of team development, individuals work well with each other to overcome obstacles in order to move the team along towards its mission. Disagreements and problems are resolved professionally and the overall effort of the team is much more coordinated than at previous stages. Team members are extremely motivated during the production phase and commitment is at its highest. Members of teams that are able to stay in the *Performing Stage* of development for extended periods of time enjoy greater fulfillment. These members evaluate their individual performance in relation to the team's performance and enjoy tremendous personal growth from their experience.

When a team is performing well, its members begin to look at the performance and evaluate why things are working and what could be better. When this occurs, new leadership roles develop and the dynamics of the group shift as tasks shift. This marks the final stage of team development, Stage 3, *Reforming*.

Stage 3—Reforming

Often, when teams reach their goals they face disbanding or severe changes to membership. This can cause much stress and sadness among the group's original members as they realize the emptiness they will feel without the support of their group. Many teams will look to find other projects or to continue their original projects, if possible, just to keep the team intact. Other teams lose members or accept new members as their goals change or their responsibilities increase. Some teams will rotate between performing and reforming for years. The process of winding down successful projects, looking for new projects, assimilating new members, losing other members, or ending the team's existence is considered *Reforming*, and represents the final stage of development for a team.

Practice:

Since early stages of team development are usually accompanied by tension and anxiety, what can the team's leader do to help members adjust?

Possible Answer:

Team leaders can do any of the following at the team's first meeting to ensure that the members start on the right foot and have a chance to get acquainted.

1. Hold an orientation session where members do exercises to learn about each other and share information. For example, one such exercise is the *interview*. Team members are grouped into pairs and each person interviews the other person asking standard questions that include background information, expectations for their team involvement, and some pertinent experiences. The partners then introduce each other to the rest of the team—sharing the information they gathered.

2. Hold a goal-setting session where the team works together to define its mission and set goals.

3. Break the group into sub-groups of two or three people and pose an important question. Have the sub-groups work on answers, then *sell* those answers to the rest of the team.

TEAM NORMS

The standards for behavior and attitudes that develop as a result of the settling in phase of team development can be called "team norms." Team norms basically serve as the rules for acceptance within the team. They are the guidelines that define what it means to be a productive member of the team. They clarify what values are integral to the team's success. While these norms do not have to be written, they are always understood by a majority of the members, and once they are accepted, they allow the team to work as a true team and they guide the team's performance.

Since team norms are the blueprints for success within a team, you can be a better team member if you help the team form positive norms that will have a lasting effect on performance. Knowing how team norms develop within a group can help you participate in their formation.

Team norms can be:

1. brought in from an individuals' past experiences,

2. born within the group, or

3. invented from a member of the group (often the leader).

Experiences from the Past Can Help Create Team Norms

Obviously, members who have worked on a team before often bring norms from their past team experience to their new team. For instance, if you learned in high school, during your participation on the football team or on the staff of the school newspaper, that "one for all, and all for one" is an excellent value for team members to live by, then you will try to make this a key value in any subsequent team. On the other hand, if you were part of team whose members constantly stole from each other and back-stabbed at every turn, you might bring a different set of values with you and you will try to establish those values as team norms.

Team Norms Can Be Born from within the Group

Often, norms are born of behaviors that take place early in the group's formation—whether they are positive or negative, planned or unplanned. For example, if a team's members happen to agree on a key point during the orientation phase and they decide to put the issue to a quick vote because they want to move on, they have planted the seed for democracy to be a team norm. It is likely that subsequent decision-making tasks will be voted on and a "majority rules" attitude will be a strong norm for the team.

Individual Members Can Invent Team Norms

Norms can also be invented by a group member, usually in the *Forming Stage* or early in the *Performing Stage*. Often team leaders or members who are well respected can make a public statement to the team that either causes other members to change their perspective or has a positive impact on the dynamics of the group and therefore becomes ingrained as a team norm. For instance, if your team is stagnated at a particular point in a project because members can't stop arguing about decisions that were made in the last meeting, and one of the team's more outspoken members stands up, commands the attention of the entire group, and declares, "Yesterday is gone! We must focus today on what will make tomorrow better!", from that point on in the team's existence, the focus may be on moving ahead, not questioning what was done in the past. This team norm was invented by the comments made by a team member.

CHAPTER SUMMARY

- All teams go through similar stages of development, which include periods of forming, performing, and reforming.

- Team norms are key values that guide behaviors and attitudes for the team.

- Positive team norms can help a team effectively progress through the different stages of development and reach a state of cohesion and unity.

Skill Building

If you are a part of a team, either at work or in your personal life, try to list what you consider to be the team norms. At what stage of development is your team? What can you do to positively affect the growth development of your team?

CHAPTER | 14

TEAM MEMBER ROLES

LEARNING OBJECTIVES

After reading this chapter you should be able to identify:

- positive team roles that help accomplish the team's task or help build unity

- negative team roles that stall progress and cause friction within the team

TEAM MEMBERS TAKE ON DIFFERENT ROLES

As members search for a comfortable identity within a team, they may stick with carrying out roles they have mastered in other group situations or they may move in and out of roles that fit better within the current group. While it would make sense that members looking for belonging and worth within the team would gravitate towards empowering roles that lead to team success, this is not always the case. Often a team's members carry out roles that reflect negative past experiences. Or members may not realize that their negative behavior is hurting the team, and that they have a choice to act in a more positive way.

By knowing about team member roles you can have a positive impact on your team, and by knowing who is playing what roles within a team, you can curb the troublemakers and encourage the builders. You can help you minimize the negative effects of those members acting out negative roles because you can "catch" them and perhaps help them move into more positive roles. On the other hand, you can also help maximize the effects of those members carrying out positive roles by reinforcing their behavior. Knowing what roles can be healthy for a team and what roles can be destructive will help you find roles that you are comfortable in and that help build the team.

Task Champion Roles

Task champions take on task-oriented team building roles. Their behavior helps move the team along by focusing time and energy on the tasks required for the team to meet its goals. *Task champions* get the job done, while reinforcing unity by focusing on the team's mission. There are many different types of *task champions*. The following list describes each type and gives examples.

Initiator
proposes new ideas to accomplish tasks, good at starting the problem solving process if the problem being addressed is task-oriented and can be overcome by doing something. Example: Jon, in the *initiator* role, tells the group, "The only way we can possibly get this project done in time is to break it up into three separate tasks and break the group up into three separate subgroups, each focused on one of the tasks. I'll take care of . . . ."

Investigator
always seeks the facts, will ask questions of everyone in order to uncover hidden clues, missing pieces of information, and like a good investigator, will remain objective or neutral throughout the questioning, reserving judgment

for a committee or for someone else. Example: Carla, asserting her role as the *investigator*, replies, "Jon, why do you think we need to break the team into three groups? How do you think we should do it, I mean, who should be in what subgroup?"

Pawn

Like the pawn in the game of chess, is always willing to pave the way so tasks can be accomplished. Members in the role of *pawn* don't have to be the most skilled in the task at hand, yet they are the first to jump in and start doing, once the *initiator* breaks the ice. Example: Michael, always the first to jump in once the pool is open says, "Yeah great, I'll be in your group Stacy. What do you want me to work on first? I could do this or maybe get started on that."

Synthesizer

Waits until many ideas are being discussed and then organizes the ideas into a coherent, unified solution. *Synthesizers* summarize the current ideas and then draw conclusions based on a little of this idea and a little of that idea. Often these members are the heavy thinkers who may not always come up with the ideas themselves, but who take ideas that don't seem to have any connection and put them together to make sense. Example: Selena, with her hands in the air motioning for everyone to listen up, finally speaks. "You know, if we take what Charlie just said, and then apply what Nell was talking about earlier and each of the subgroups can trade the results, we could probably get this thing done well before it's due."

Producer

Puts the requisite energy and effort into accomplishing the tasks at hand. Every team member should be able to slide into the role of *producer* at one point or another. When tasks involve everyone pitching in to get the job done, *producers* go to work to get the job done. Example: Once the tasks were clearly defined for each subgroup, even team members who had been quiet or non-participative during the morning's discussion could be seen working hard on the project in the afternoon. Every member was carrying out her role as *producer*.

Social Champions

Social champions take on social or emotional team building roles. Their behavior helps move the team along by focusing time and energy on the social and emotional needs of the team. *Social champions* help *task champions* get the job done by strengthening the unity of the team through supportive and reinforcing behavior. The following list describes the various types of *social champion*s and gives examples of their behavior.

Supporter

Encourages ideas by making members feel good about participating. Supporters often praise ideas and build commitment to the team through positive reinforcement. Example: You always hear *supporters* saying 'good job,' 'well done,' 'I like that idea,' 'way to go,' etc.

Facilitator

Convinces other members to join the discussion. *Facilitators* will draw out ideas from members who may not offer their suggestions on their own. They get everyone talking. Example: Jenny noticed that neither Bret nor Carly had said anything regarding the new plan. Playing the role of *facilitator*, she remarked, 'I really think that this is a good idea and we should follow the plan as Phil described. Carly, doesn't this plan sound good? Bret, do you agree with Carly?'

Peacemaker

Reconciles conflict and builds areas of agreement between members who are not seeing eye-to-eye. *Peacemakers* are similar to *synthesizers*, but their focus isn't on the best plan for a given task, but rather on a best plan for a meeting of the minds. *Peacemakers* will take heated discussions and reword or reformulate the argument to draw parallels and make connections so the parties work together towards a solution instead of against each other. Some peacemakers are even able to mediate between two parties who have escalated an argument to the point where they can't even talk to each other. Example: After Carly and Bret argued for five minutes about how their respective plans were better for the team and the other's wouldn't work, Jermaine jumped in and asked Carly and Bret if she could summarize what their plans were and what she thought were the real differences between the two. In summarizing the two plans, she highlighted the areas where they overlapped and changed each plan just a little to make them work together. Afterward both Bret and Carly agreed that their plans weren't that far apart and that Jermaine's idea to use the best of both plans would be the best solution for the team. Jermaine clearly acted as a *peacemaker*.

"Norm"inator

Confronts members who act outside of the team's accepted norms. *Norminators*, or *Norm Police*, attack and destroy undesirable behavior by pointing it out in front of the group and threatening to take action to punish the members who display such behavior. *Norminators* are like wardens; they can be your best friend if your behavior is good, but if you act irresponsibly or cause trouble, they are your worst nightmare. Some groups nominate a warden or a *norminator*, giving them official power to carrier out this important role. Example: Having heard enough from the troublemaker Phil, Scott jumped to his feet, stood over Phil's chair, and in a deep, loud voice shouted, "We will not hear any more of this! If you don't have anything constructive to say and your behavior doesn't change, you will be removed from this room immediately!"

Compromiser

Agrees with others and even shifts his/her own opinion to agree with the consensus in order to maintain unity within the group. A group that has too many *compromisers* operates with very little tension but makes sub-optimal decisions due to a general lack of differences of opinion. However, a few *compromisers* in a team can make for smoother discussions and can serve to ease tension. Example: Senator James says about the vote, "I'll vote yes just to move things along, even though I don't really understand or agree with this bill." Hearing his comments, Senators Hook and Straw simultaneously reply, "I'll second that sentiment—I vote yes. Yes, for me too."

Counselor

Monitors the collective behavior of the team's members and makes recommendations to help keep the social atmosphere positive. The counselor will address issues that affect the dynamics of the group, keeping a keen focus on such elements as cohesiveness, cooperation, commitment, and motivation, whether or not they affect the task at hand. The counselor is often proactive as well, pointing out where things are going right and helping avoid negative behavior. Example: Jennifer, clearly in a counselor role, remarks, "I have been listening to this debate for over an hour, and I really feel that the reason we haven't accepted Ron's view is because we are afraid to go against Mark, who has done such a great job as the team's leader. If you look at the process here, it seems that every time we get close to a vote for Ron's idea, someone starts talking about how good a job Mark has done. Let's decide as a team whether Ron's idea merits going against what has become the norm—accepting Mark's plans all the time."

Practice:

Read through the list of *task-champion* roles and think of times when you were on a team and played any of these key roles. Write them down and think how you would play the same role on a current team or in the office.

Task Inhibitors

Not all team member roles are positive. *Task inhibitors* exhibit task-oriented team-subverting roles. Their behavior inhibits the progress of the group to accomplish its tasks. *Task inhibitors* can act out against their teammates in many ways: some openly exhibit behavior that stifles unity and teamwork, while others subtly stir up discontent. The following list describes several *Task inhibitor* roles and gives examples.

Dominator

Takes over the lead in a discussion regardless of whether he is qualified to lead. *Dominators* rarely seek other opinions or invite others to participate and even when other members try to get their *two cents* in, the *dominator* will act as if nothing was said and just keep right on blabbing. *Dominators* come in degrees; some always have to try to be in charge, while others merely have to speak their mind on every single issue, even if their input is no different than ideas already discussed. Example: Maria spoke for 45 minutes out of the hour and barely even let anyone else talk. When other members raised objections or asked her questions about her plan, she basically blew them off, didn't address their questions, and kept right on selling her plan.

Naysayer

Uses many ways to stop progress right in its tracks. Sometimes *naysayers* can trick the team by using the tactic of making soft or noncommittal agreement statements and then subtly inserting a *but* into their argument, after which heavy criticism is launched to convince the team not to support the idea. Other times *naysayers* can be direct and just say no. Whatever their method, be it straightforward or trickery, the *naysayer* always manages to find fault— in everything. Example: Halfway into the vote, Marcus remarked, "We shouldn't proceed with Nancy's plan because the following things are wrong . . . ." Two hours later, when a new plan was devised, Marcus spoke up again, "No, no, no. We can't possibly do this because . . . ."

Detractor

Like *naysayers*, criticize every plan or idea. *Detractors*, however, gripe and moan as if their purpose was to be the team's official whiner. *Detractors* have to find fault in everything because, in general, they just can't be happy or satisfied. Example: Clive, after making that sour face that everyone has grown accustomed to, spoke up. "But we always do what Phil wants. The last time we listened to Phil and had that car-wash it rained all day. And the time before that was the walk-a-thon that was canceled because of Hurricane Edwardo. I say we don't plan any activities for outside, especially if Phil suggests it."

Free Rider

Doesn't do any work and is never prepared. Often *free riders* can keep their position on a team because they defend the odd ideas and win a few supporters along the way, as members who need at least one person to side with defend them in front of the group. Example: Jonathan has done no work on the team's website despite threats from the project leader that he will be forced to start over next semester with another team. Stephen, however, keeps putting pressure on other members to look the other way as far as Jonathan's inactivity is concerned, because Jonathan is one of three people that will vote for Stephen's choice of formatting for the FAQs page. Jonathan, clearly a *free rider*, continues to be a part of the team, despite the fact that he doesn't do any of the work that he is supposed to.

Digressor

Always takes the conversation somewhere else. Whether caused by a short attention span, a lack of focus, or an inability to connect one idea to another, the *digressor* will almost always take the focus of the group away from the task at hand. Unless members catch them quickly and curb their behavior, *digressors* can render any team ineffective. Example: The rest of the team winced when the guest speaker called on Cheryl, because they knew, somehow, some way, she would find a way to tell the same story about how her old boss treated her unfairly, how she would never let anyone buy her a drink, and about the time she saw the mayor run a red light.

Social Malcontents

Take on social or emotional team-subverting roles. Their behavior hinders group cohesion because they undermine the team building activities and the focus on positive attitudes by attacking members' ideas and making the attacks personal. *Social malcontents* can take on several roles.

Instigator

Always on the attack, not so much on other's ideas, but on them personally. *Instigators* have to start fights, even if they are not involved in the fight. Example: An *instigator* would say, 'Mary, did you hear what Theo said about your proposal? Well, if I weren't a gentleman I would tell you exactly what he said, but I would rather not repeat that kind of language. Who does he think he is anyway? And besides, I think your work is just fine.'

Labeller

Has to put a label on everybody, even if the label doesn't apply. Some members, in order to avoid real communication or having to deal with their own emotions, will put labels on other members. As you know, once labels and stereotypes are used, the communication process can be altered and the dynamics of the team certainly suffer. Example: "Mona, you always put men down. Why don't you just admit that you are a man-hating feminist?"

Shmoozer

Loves to make members feel comfortable just for the sake of being their temporary friend. Shmoozers are dangerous because they can lull you into a false sense of security. They 'yes' your ideas to death, but really don't know or don't care whether they are good ideas at all. They just want you to like them. They are part of the team to be in the social environment and often couldn't care less about the tasks that need to be accomplished. Example: Dominique says to Tony: "Yes Tony, I think that's a great idea—you should run for club president. You got my vote." Tony leaves the room. Dominique then tells Liza: " I hope you're thinking about running for president, because your ideas are the best. I'm voting for you all the way."

Practice

If you can remember playing any of these negative roles within a team, think about why you behaved as you did and what you could do differently in the same situation to avoid inhibiting progress.

CHAPTER SUMMARY

- Team members can exhibit many roles throughout the existence of the team.
- Members can take on positive roles that help accomplish the tasks at hand or help strengthen the cohesiveness of the team.
- Some members take on negative roles within the team and stop or stall progress towards the tasks or cause friction among members.

Skill Building

Notice how people in your office can take on team member roles. Try to see if you can identify a person for each role in your office. Hint: some people will take on many roles.

CHAPTER | 15

LEADERSHIP AND TEAMS

LEARNING OBJECTIVES

After reading this chapter you should be able to:

- set SMART team goals
- identify key roles and traits that make a team leader successful

WHERE DO TEAM LEADERS COME FROM?

Team leaders are either appointed or they emerge from within the group. When appointed, team leaders can be chosen from within the group or from outside the team and they are usually selected because of their traits, skills, knowledge, ability to work with the team members, or their position. When a leader emerges from within the team it is mostly because he or she has demonstrated strong leadership skills. Either way, once in a leadership position, the roles and responsibilities are similar for both an appointed leader and an emergent leader. Every team leader needs to guide her team to the point where its members can work cohesively together to accomplish shared goals.

SETTING SMART GOALS

Since most workplace teams are set up for a purpose, whether to solve an important business problem, evaluate a new opportunity, or deliver a project (perform certain tasks), it is the leader's ultimate responsibility to make sure that the team's purpose is realized. No matter what the purpose, the only way to effectively let team members know what is expected of them is by setting SMART team goals. In order for a team to be successful, the members need to start on the same page and continuously know where they are going and if they are getting there. SMART goals help teams work more effectively because members understand and own their team's goals while team leaders can have a baseline—the goals—to evaluate performance against.

SMART team goals are **S**pecific, **M**utual, **A**ttainable, **R**ewarded, and tied to a definite **T**imeline.

Specific

Team goals should be specific and measurable (when applicable). While not every goal can be quantifiable or expressed in real numbers, every goal should be as precise as possible, and give the team a way to measure progress.

Example: An ineffective goal for a customer-service team would be "to improve the turn-around time for customer complaint response letters," while a specific and measurable goal would be "to decrease the turn-around time for all customer complaint response letters by 50% and to achieve an average turn-around time of under 24-hours for all responses handled by the group."

Mutual

Team goals should be the result of mutual agreement. Members show much higher levels of commitment towards a goal that they help set. All members should, therefore, participate in the goal-setting process, rather than be handed down a list of objectives from a leader or manager.

Attainable

All goals should be attainable and challenging. If goals are too easy, motivation levels can be low, but if goals are unreasonable then the team is set up for failure—which can cause morale, motivation, and commitment problems. In order to set challenging yet realistic goals, all available resources must be surveyed and reflected in the goals.

> Example: "The goal for this department is for every employee to work an average of 90 hours over the course of this holiday season" is certainly not an attainable or realistic goal for most employees. A more effective goal would be: "The goal for this department is to outsell all other departments by 50%, even if our overtime pay surpasses our regular pay."

Rewarded

When rewards are linked to goals, those goals have much more meaning and motivational power than goals that have no rewards. It is human nature to seek rewards for accomplishments. Rewards can be given in many ways, but the most effective rewards for a team's goals are those that can be easily shared by every member. Rewards that serve as a bonding experience for the members are extremely effective.

For example, a party or team excursion would be a very effective reward for a team that achieves its goals, because the reward can be shared by the whole team, and can serve as a venue for building even stronger ties between members.

Time Focused

Goals should be clear about the time period over which they will be achieved. Without a defined time-frame or a deadline, realizing the goals and rewarding them can be very difficult.

> Example: By Friday of next week, our group should have closed 14 new accounts.

Practice:

Think of something that you wish to accomplish within the next month. Set a SMART goal regarding that accomplishment.

Answer:

Answers will vary. Check to make sure that your goal is Specific, Measurable, Attainable and Challenging, Rewarded, and Time specific.

HOW DOES A LEADER GET HER TEAM TO WORK AS A PRODUCTIVE UNIT?

There is an old saying that goes, *If you give a man a fish you will feed him for a day, but if you teach him to fish he will feed himself for the rest of his life.* Today, team leaders are realizing the same thing. The modern translation is: If you lead a team by asserting power and by manipulating the members to achieve results, you may reach your goals once, but that's it. However, if you lead a team by giving the members the power to make their own decisions and by cultivating commitment and motivation through trust and open communication, your team will be successful even in your absence.

In today's business environment, as you will recall from chapter 1 of this book, *Learning organizations* are changing the way they do business to better make use of their talent pool, where employees are fewer but smarter and trained in business skills such as problem solving and teamwork. To lead a group of talented individuals who have these advanced skills, today's team leaders and managers have to be dynamic coaches, mentors, facilitators, and performers.

The remainder of this chapter will focus on the roles that team leaders take to advance the social and developmental needs of the team while managing the specific tasks required to meet the team's performance goals.

TEAM LEADER TRAITS

In order for person to be an effective team leader, she should possess certain traits.

Team leaders are:

- Driven—they need to achieve, their energy level is always high, and their initiative is strong.

- Motivated by Leadership—they inherently seek to empower others to help them reach personal and team goals.

- Confident—they know that they don't know everything and they trust their ability to get the best out of others.

- Open—they share information on a professional and personal level. They are honest, trustworthy, and work with a high level of integrity.

- Intelligent—they integrate and interpret large amounts of information and facilitate problem-solving and decision-making activities.

- Original—they use their creativity and flexibility to adapt to many different situations and to fulfill multiple requirements.

- Visionaries—they can look ahead and envision what the team will be like and do the right things along the way to get it there.

TEAM LEADER ROLES

Team leaders take on many roles within their teams. As you will remember from chapter 13, a team goes through many distinct phases of development. Teams get more productive as their members work with each other and become a unit. During a team's development, the ultimate job of a team leader is to facilitate the progress of the team's social and task skills: to help it along the path towards cohesion and production. When you assume the role of team leader, you must adapt during different stages of development and take on appropriate roles for specific situations.

LEADERSHIP ROLES IN THE FORMATION STAGE OF TEAM DEVELOPMENT

In the early stages of team development a team leader will take active leadership roles, directing members through exercises for the first time and demonstrating positive roles by leading discussions and problem-solving and decision-making tasks.

In the early stages of team development, leaders will often perform the roles of *initiator, investigator, supporter,* and *facilitator.* She will actively direct the communication process; asking questions, using active listening skills, and pursuing involvement from all team members. The leader will lead the team through problem-solving and decision-making tasks, ensuring that each member participates and has a chance to offer relevant knowledge and information.

A team leader will work very hard in the early stages of team development to make sure that the team's members all participate in establishing the goals of the team. As the team moves through the early stages of development, the leader will work with individual members to make sure they are comfortable and confident in their own roles and that their roles serve the goals of the team. The leader will also serve the *norminator* role, acting as the watchdog to protect team norms.

LEADERSHIP ROLES IN THE PERFORMING STAGE OF TEAM DEVELOPMENT

As the team advances into more mature stages of development, the team leader will take passive leadership roles, coaching members through exercises and facilitating discussions and decision-making and problem-solving tasks instead of leading them. During this stage of development, the leader will take on roles such as *facilitator, synthesizer,* and *counselor.*

LEADERSHIP ROLES IN THE REFORMING STAGE OF TEAM DEVELOPMENT

Once a team advances through the different stages of development and becomes a cohesive unit that can realize its goals without the active help of its leader, the leader serves as a *consultant* or an *advisor*. As either a consultant or advisor, the team leader is present for any help the team may seek, but offers very little in terms of proactive advise or direction. At this point, the team leader may serve in a *mentor* role, helping shape the team's new emergent leader.

TEAM LEADERS FOCUS ON *SOFT SKILLS*

Team leaders focus on *soft skills* in order to ensure social growth and team cohesion. They must, themselves, demonstrate these behaviors, as well as teach them to their group.

Communicating

Team leaders need to communicate well. They are the role models, and members frequently imitate their behavior. When team leaders communicate, they always use active listening skills and make effective use of constructive feedback.

Resolving Conflict

Since all teams go through periods marked by conflict, it is up to the team leader to take charge and make sure the team goes through the proper channels to resolve conflict in a constructive and lasting manner. If the team leader is unfamiliar with effective conflict resolution techniques and tries to avoid dealing with conflict, the team will not develop as well as it should.

Problem Solving

Team leaders need to use effective group problem-solving techniques. Solving problems using critical thinking skills is important for team leaders, who must not only solve problems on their own but must also help team members solve individual problems and group problems. Teams can be very successful solving problems and evaluating opportunities if all members are given the chance to participate and the proper techniques are used to ensure quality decisions. It is the team leader's responsibility to implement effective team problem-solving techniques.

Motivating Members

In the early stages of team development, members lose their motivation and unity is usually very low. A team leader needs to motivate members even when the situation has little or no apparent motivators. Team leaders need to work with members to clarify and strengthen their individual roles within the team and to manage their expectations in order to motivate them.

Building Trust

Without trust a team will never reach a state of cohesion. At the very nature of collaboration and teamwork lies trust. A team leader has to build trust between herself and the members, as well as between the members. Setting up open communication channels and using continuous objective feedback can help a team leader foster trust within the team.

Sharing

Sharing and building trust go hand in hand in creating an atmosphere where communication is open and team experiences are rich. Team leaders have to share information, power, praise, and responsibilities in order to facilitate the growth of the team. As a role model, the team leader who hides or guards information will not motivate his team.

CHAPTER SUMMARY

- Team leaders use SMART goals to manage team performance and motivate team members.

- Team leaders share similar leadership traits that help them successfully work in a dynamic environment and they focus on *soft skills* such as communication, conflict resolution, motivating others, building trust, and sharing.

- Team leaders adapt their work style and play different roles during the development of their team, moving from directors to facilitators and coaches and then serving as mentors or consultants when the team has developed into a cohesive unit.

Skill Building

Have you ever been a team leader? If you have, then use this worksheet to evaluate your strengths and weaknesses as a team leader. If you haven't, use this worksheet to evaluate the strengths and weaknesses of a team leader that you have worked with.

SKILL OR TRAIT	RATE YOUR ABILITY IN OR APTITUDE FOR PERFORMING			
Set SMART Goals	Always	Sometimes	Never	Needs Improvement
Driven	Always	Sometimes	Never	Needs Improvement
Motivated by Leadership	Always	Sometimes	Never	Needs Improvement
Confident	Always	Sometimes	Never	Needs Improvement
Open	Always	Sometimes	Never	Needs Improvement
Intelligent	Always	Sometimes	Never	Needs Improvement
Original	Always	Sometimes	Never	Needs Improvement
Visionary	Always	Sometimes	Never	Needs Improvement
Communicating	Always	Sometimes	Never	Needs Improvement
Resolving Conflict	Always	Sometimes	Never	Needs Improvement
Problem Solving	Always	Sometimes	Never	Needs Improvement
Motivating Members	Always	Sometimes	Never	Needs Improvement
Building Trust	Always	Sometimes	Never	Needs Improvement
Sharing	Always	Sometimes	Never	Needs Improvement

CHAPTER | 16

COMMUNICATING EFFECTIVELY IN TEAMS

LEARNING OBJECTIVES

After reading this chapter you should be able to communicate more effectively in a team by:

- giving constructive feedback
- using assertive communication techniques

SUCCESSFUL TEAMS VALUE OPEN COMMUNICATION

In order for teams to be effective and cohesive units, working together towards a common goal, open communication has to be valued by every member. Members should feel free to say what they mean, and mean what they say. Successful teams encourage feedback and their members share emotions in a professional and constructive manner.

The following section outlines key values and practices utilized by effective teams to foster team unity through constructive communication.

Trust, Respect, and Openness

In order to create a team atmosphere where communication is open and free-flowing, trust must prevail. Members must be able to trust that other members will respect their rights to express ideas and feelings. Individuals need to feel that they can trust that others are doing the work they are supposed to. In essence, those who work together in a team need to trust that all members hold the same values and, above all else, serve the team's goals.

Trust can only be earned. While you can give someone the benefit of the doubt that they deserve your trust, or you, theirs, that only sets up a forum for the trust to be earned. Once members start to earn each other's trust regarding work ethics, team tasks, and team norms, they begin to share information and feedback much more freely. They converse openly, not worrying as much about impressing other members or guarding their personal feelings. When levels of trust and respect for each other are high, the resulting openness in communications can foster creativity and lead a team to high performance and unity.

Handling Emotions

While most business communications should limit the inclusion of emotions and personal feelings, it is almost impossible to limit such factors in a team environment. Communications among team members will almost always include emotionally-charged language based on personal feelings and not objective viewpoints.

How can you curb this type of communication in a team?

The answer: You can't, and you probably shouldn't. Instead, you should make sure that every team member is aware of the difference between objective viewpoints and subjective feelings. Actually, once team members are aware of the difference, expressing emotions can be an effective team building tool. Communication that deals with emotions as emotions, and not as fact or objective reality, can serve to unify a team. Often emotions and personal feelings are necessary for members to fully explain their perspective or share their point of view. Once emotions are expressed and an open discussion is held regarding the personal feelings of team members, all members can better focus on the team's mission, goals, and tasks.

Giving Constructive Feedback

Another important and often emotionally-charged aspect of team communication is feedback. Feedback is essential to effective teamwork. How can members learn about their own needs and help others discover areas that need improvement without feedback? Feedback is the tool that lets members communicate to each other about performance, behaviors, and attitudes. Since feedback can be emotionally-charged, teams need to actively manage feedback and keep it constructive.

Here are a few guidelines:

Giving and receiving feedback should be an important part of the team's norms.

Without feedback it is virtually impossible to improve the way you work together. Team members should be aware of the important role feedback can play in the growth of the team, and constructive feedback should be encouraged and accepted by all members.

Feedback should be used for positive reinforcement, not just to point out areas of concern or problems.

Too many people think that feedback is only for expressing problems or concerns. What about congratulating someone for a good effort or pointing out when someone does a great job or says something important? Feedback needs to include positive reinforcement. Positive feedback will not only give energy and higher self-esteem to those who receive it, it will also serve to legitimize the negative feedback. Team members will pay more attention to your concerns if they also hear you compliment someone once in awhile.

Constructive feedback should follow a specific formula and all team members should be aware of and have experience with the formula.

The following tips can be used for managing constructive feedback, whether the feedback is positive or negative.

1. Be clear from the start that you are describing a personal opinion or expressing an emotion (when applicable), by prefacing your feedback with an "I" statement.

   As you may remember from chapter 7, using *I* and not *you* is a good tool to reduce the tension and alleviate the defensiveness that often results from accusations. For example, if you need to give a team member feedback about his annoying habit of always cutting the speaker off, instead of saying, 'You always cut people off and that has to stop,' you could be more diplomatic and probably get better results by saying, 'I feel annoyed when you cut me off and I am speaking. I also feel bothered when you cut other people off because I think that you are not respecting them as members who have important things to say.'

2. Be descriptive and thorough in your observations.

   While you may be expressing your opinions or your emotions regarding an event or a particular subject, you are also describing specific behaviors and actions that have occurred. When describing these actions or behaviors it is important to be as specific as possible, including as many details as appropriate. It is also important to include shared examples that all members can relate to. For instance, continuing the example from above, 'And I know that when I was talking about the changes that we made to the team's website and then you jumped in and began discussing your ideas for a new fund raiser, I was annoyed, because . . .'

3. Don't use labels or stereotypes in your feedback.

   While a label such as disrespectful may be an accurate way to describe the behavior of the member in the example above, labels should be discouraged when giving constructive feedback. The problem with labels is that, although they describe the behavior that is in question, they usually stick to the person, regardless of whether or not they are accurate. It is much better to address the behavior without the use of a label. The example above describes the behavior as disrespectful without putting the label on the team member.

4. Don't exaggerate and speak for yourself.

Be exact, use qualifiers such as *last time* or *twice*, and don't use absolutes like *never* and *always* when giving feedback. Stay away from generalizing your comments to include the whole team. Speak for yourself. Your comments are yours and no one else's. You lose credibility with other members if you often exaggerate your claims or speak on behalf of the team. For example, the wrong way to give the feedback in the example from above would be to say, 'You always cut people off, and everyone is upset.'

Practice:

At an important meeting, a member of your product development team, Jan, has offered to represent the team by attending an upcoming trade show. You think that she wants to go to the trade show in Chicago because that is where she went to college and has many friends there. You don't think that Jan is the best member to represent the team. Another member, Sharma, has worked for the competition—which will be unveiling their new line of products at the trade show. You think Sharma should represent the team, not Jan, because Sharma can best position your product against her old company's products at the show. Your teammates respect your opinion on most important decisions and you are usually the leader when it comes to taking an authoritative position. You need to speak up now, as the team will be voting to send someone to the trade show any minute. How do you best give Jan feedback on her request and position Sharma to be your delegate in a constructive manner?

Possible Answer:

'Jan, while I respect your talents and would like to give you a chance to see your friends in Chicago, I feel that Sharma would be a more effective representative for our products at the trade show. I believe that Sharma's years at Riverhead Technologies [the competitors] will give her an edge in selling our products against theirs, and that could be quite good for the whole team, because our goal for the trade show is to convince the attending buyers that our products are not only as good as Riverhead's but they are better. Don't you think that Sharma's presence at the trade show would give us a tremendous advantage against Riverhead, and help us accomplish our goal?'

Constructive Feedback Using Assertive Communication

Assertiveness training is offered by many consulting firms and endorsed by the American Management Association as a means to effective communications. A team can benefit greatly if its members are familiar with assertive communication techniques.

Assertive communication reflects each member's right to express their needs, their feelings or emotions, and their desires for change in others. Unlike aggressive behavior, assertive behavior implies that you also respect the same rights of others. Aggressive communicators don't care about the feelings or rights of others, they just want to get their point across and will do so at any cost.

While assertive communication shares many of the traits that the constructive feedback guidelines above have already covered, these techniques are important for effective team communication and bear repeating. Assertive communicators:

- Respect the rights of others
    - Each member has a right to express his feelings, opinions, needs, and desires.
    - Each member has a right to seek change in other's behavior if it is deemed destructive.

- — Comments and criticism are confined to behaviors and attitudes and are not made as attacks on the individual.

- Give the facts and use concrete examples

  - — Situations are described with specific details and objectivity.

  - — Recent examples are always used.

- Express feelings in a friendly and professional manner

  - — When expressing a situation the assertive communicator relates his feelings about that situation by clearly announcing opinions, emotions, needs, and desires as his own.

- Invite feedback from others

  - — Communication is two-way and others have a right to give their feedback to correct information and include their feelings, opinions, needs, and desires.

- Clearly describe the behavior changes they seek as well as the benefits

  - — When seeking change in other's behavior, assertive communicators clearly describe the behavior that they would like to see.

  - — They also describe the benefits that the team will enjoy if the behavior is changed.

- Accept that their own behavior may need adjustment

  - — When her own behavior has not been effective or has drawn criticism the assertive communicator accepts responsibility and attempts to make the necessary changes.

CHAPTER SUMMARY

Effective Teams:

- respect the rights of all members to freely communicate their feelings, opinions, and attitudes in an open and professional environment.

- use constructive feedback and assertive communication techniques to maintain a professional atmosphere and build team unity.

Skill Building

Does your office or your work team use constructive feedback techniques to build unity and progress towards its goals? If yes, list three ways you can help others use these tools. If no, how can you start to use these tools to be a better employee?

CHAPTER | 17

RESOLVING TEAM CONFLICT

LEARNING OBJECTIVES

After reading this chapter you should be able to:

- create team norms that will have a positive effect on the team's ability to resolve conflict

- communicate effectively when you are involved in a conflict with another team member

- serve as a productive team member in situations where conflict must be resolved

CONFLICTS ARE ESSENTIAL TO TEAM DEVELOPMENT

Most teams will experience conflict, but the question is whether or not they resolve it in a positive manner. Successful teams know that resolving conflict is the key to their success. Teams that use effective communication techniques and are prepared to deal with conflict in a professional and friendly manner will use conflict to strengthen their unity. Teams that do not communicate effectively and are not prepared for conflict will either let it blow up and cause real damage to the team's unity or will suppress it until it degrades relationships and surfaces as harmful or hostile attitudes and behaviors.

Why is conflict so prevalent in teams?

One of the factors that makes a team productive and provides for a rich experience for its members is the diversity of its membership. Teams are not usually made up of a group of homogenous individuals (people with the same backgrounds, experiences, knowledge, or attitudes). This diversity means that there are lots of different personalities and differing perspectives or points of view on a team. Whenever you have a group of diverse people all trying to communicate with one another you will certainly have a few differences in opinion or clashing views. These differences often result in an argument, and when arguments escalate, they result in conflict.

Other factors that cause members to argue and can lead to conflict include: stress; unclear objectives, responsibilities, or procedures; miscommunication; external anger or unmet needs being projected onto the team; inappropriate emotions; uncertainty about the future of the job or the team; competing personal needs; or poor leadership.

How can teams avoid conflict? They can't, and they shouldn't.

PREPARE FOR CONFLICT

Teams need to avoid escalating conflict, not conflict itself. Instead of trying to avoid conflict, teams should instead prepare for handling it in a positive way, because conflict can help a team grow by strengthening the communication skills of their members and helping build team unity.

The best way to prepare a team for handling conflict in a positive manner is to train the members in constructive feedback practices and assertive communication techniques. Prevention is the best cure in this case, because if a team is prepared to deal with differing opinions and arguments by using constructive feedback and/or assertive communication techniques then the chances are relatively high that conflict will not escalate. Refer back to chapter 16 and review the characteristics of constructive feedback and assertive communication.

The following are several key norms that can help set the right attitude and atmosphere in a team so that conflict resolution can be a positive experience.

Key Norms Regarding Conflict Resolution

- Conflict is a part of teamwork and should be dealt with like any other team issue.

- Conflict is about issues, not people.

- Conflict when managed with honesty, integrity, and openness can lead to team growth and make the team stronger.

- Conflict is an opportunity to build communication skills and to improve the cohesiveness of the team.

- Conflict resolution is future oriented: what has already happened is done; what is important now is what has to be done to make sure that the same thing doesn't happen in the future.

RESOLVING CONFLICT

When it becomes apparent that conflict has set in, it is very important to take action right away. The team should work together to resolve the conflict. The following guidelines will help you resolve conflict within your team in a professional and constructive manner.

Tasks for the Team

1. Acknowledge that Conflict Exists and Make It a Team Issue

- If conflicts are left for individuals to deal with on their own, the team is missing an opportunity to grow in unity and to improve its overall communication skills.

- Involving the whole team will give every member an opportunity to contribute to the issue and to learn from the conflict.

- If everyone in the team learns from the discussion, chances are there won't be any more conflicts brought on by the same issue in the future.

2. Identify the Core Issues

While identifying the core issues may seem obvious and even easy, this can often be the toughest part of the resolution process.

- The key to identifying the core issues is to separate the emotional issues from the core issues.

- Draw a list of needs for each of the members involved in the conflict and make sure everyone agrees on these needs.

- Draw a list of team needs as well.

- Once the emotional issues are identified and dealt with, then the core issues need to be defined and resolved.

POSSIBLE ISSUES CAUSING CONFLICT	
Emotional Factors	*Core Issues*
• *stress*	• *unclear individual objectives or goals*
• *jealousy*	• *unclear individual roles or*
• *mood*	*responsibilities*
• *ego—competition for power*	• *unclear procedures or task directions*
or control or threats to	• *disagreements over shared values*
self-esteem	• *disagreements over team goals*
• *external anger or unmet*	• *disagreements over team leadership*
needs being projected onto	• *disagreements over facts or*
team members	*interpretation of data*
• *uncertainty about the*	• *disagreements over assignment of*
future of the job or the team	*tasks*

Practice:

Robert is one of three managers whose teams handle incoming helpline calls for a software company. On average his team handles 312 calls a day with five phone support personnel, while the other two teams handle 262 and 266 calls per day with the same number of support staff. Each team has a quota for calls of 260 per day. Lately, Robert and the other managers have been handling many calls themselves because of a new product on the market. Several new products are scheduled to be shipped next month and there is no way the current staff will be able to handle the predicted increase in calls. The vice president of customer service, Elaine Morrow, has suggested that the best way to deal with the current need is for the three managers to rotate teams, so that Robert can shape up the other two teams. Robert has agreed to the plan, as long as he is paid his bonus while he works with the other teams (he receives a bonus every week his team beats their quota by more than 10%). Elaine is in agreement, because if she can get the other two teams up to the level of Robert's team, she won't have to hire a new phone rep and the savings will reflect well on her. However, the other two managers have been openly opposed to the plan and refuse to work out the details with Robert. In fact, they have been arguing with their employees and generally miserable to each other, to Robert and Elaine, and even to some customers. They have been so preoccupied by the impending changes that their groups have missed their quotas four out of the last six days.

1. What might be the emotional issues that are affecting the two managers?

2. What are the potential core issues?

3. If you are Elaine, how can you begin to resolve the conflict that is causing chaos in your department?

Possible Answers:

1. The troubled managers could be stressed out because they have been working very hard or they could be jealous of Robert's success. More likely their stress is an ego issue: Their self-esteem could be damaged

because Robert is temporarily replacing them and they will be losing power within their own groups. They could also be unclear about their future with their teams and within the department.

2. It is hard to determine what the core issues are without more information. However, you would be safe to speculate that the managers' problems could be unclear individual objectives or goals, because according to their quotas they are meeting their goals, yet Robert is temporarily replacing them because his performance is much better. If the quota is 260 and Robert's team has a goal of 300 and the other teams have 260 as their goals, then this would support your speculation.

3. You could hold meetings with each team where the manager and their staff of five employees express their feelings regarding the intended plan and come up with alternative ways to increase their performance.

3. Moderate the Discussion

- Team members should translate what the members involved in the conflict are saying so that those members can hear what they are saying, but without the emotional attachment.

- Interpret literally. Interpreting as precisely as possible will have a stronger effect on the members involved. Avoid exaggerating views or examples—it will cause the offended party to shut off.

4. Explore Compromise and Reconciliation

- Facilitate an understanding between the parties. They may not agree with each other, but the team should be able to get them to accept and understand each other's views.

- Identify common ground.

- Look for areas where goals may overlap—highlight the team goals.

- Brainstorm for a possible solution that will reconcile the parties.

5. Agree on a Solution

- Seek agreement from both parties and the rest of the team for a solution that allows both parties to feel as if they have reconciled their differences, making sure that the team's goals have been the top priority.

- Draft an action plan to follow up the solution, making sure that all parties involved know their personal responsibilities. Include specific deadlines.

- Summarize the core issues that caused the conflict and how it was resolved.

Tasks for the Individuals Involved in Conflict

While the above steps are for the team, the following tips are for the individual members involved in the conflict.

1. Concentrate on Resolving the Core Issues

- Relax and focus on being calm and rational.

- Make sure you take at least 10 very deep breaths before you argue.

- If you are still very emotional, the tension you feel will only prevent you from communicating effectively—leave the room or situation for two minutes and focus on the core issue you need to discuss and how you think it can be resolved—not on your emotions.

2. Use Empathy

- The other person has a legitimate point of view, so if you can think of what the other person is trying to accomplish you will be better at approaching what you want, particularly as it compares to what they want.

- Compare and contrast what you are feeling to what you believe the other party is feeling. Think about how you both would like to feel when this conflict is solved—it may help you see things differently or explain things differently.

- Think of what the other team members might be thinking about the core issue.

3. Use Active Listening Skills

- Give the speaker your full attention and respect—maintain eye contact and keep a positive posture.

- Pay attention to non-verbal cues—from the other party involved in the conflict and your teammates, as well your own.

- Use verbal affirmations, ask questions, paraphrase, and reflect the implications.

- Control your emotions during the discussion, don't interrupt other speakers, and hold off on rebutting until you have heard the whole argument of the other side.

4. Defer to the Group

- The conflict may be between you and another individual, but the issue is a team issue and the team should be "in charge" of the resolution process.

- Allow other team members to intervene—they have the team's best interest as their priority and are removed from the emotions that you may have. Also, since their perspective is different than yours, they may give you enlightenment.

- Cooperate with the team's recommendations for reconciliation.

CHAPTER SUMMARY

- Conflict is an essential part of team development and should be handled positively.

- Team members have a responsibility to actively participate in conflict resolution, even when they are not involved in the conflict.

- Individuals involved in a conflict have a responsibility to work toward reconciliation in a professional and courteous manner.

Skill Building

Answer the following questions based on the last argument you were involved in at work.

1. What emotional issues were involved . . .
   — on your part?
   — for the other party?

2. What was the core issue(s)?

3. Did you resolve the conflict using any of the steps outlined in this chapter?
   — If no, what steps did you take and how do those steps fit in with those listed in this chapter?
   — If yes, which steps did you use, and could you have used others?

4. Write a summary of that conflict and summarize the core issues, and how things were resolved.

CHAPTER 18

EFFECTIVE TEAM PROBLEM SOLVING

LEARNING OBJECTIVES

After reading this chapter you should be able to:

- use the *reflective-thinking* problem-solving technique to solve personal and team problems and make better decisions
- facilitate the *reflective-thinking* problem-solving technique within a team environment

DECISION MAKING IS NOT AUTOMATIC

Problem solving and decision making are two very important processes for achieving success, whether at work or at home. When an individual makes a decision on any level, he does so by first using problem-solving or critical-thinking skills: accumulating facts about the situation; analyzing the unique circumstances; and evaluating possible actions based on the facts and analysis. During the evaluation part of the process and before a next step is chosen, the individual compares the possible decision to similar decisions that were made in the past, and to internal beliefs based on accumulated memories and feelings regarding similar and not-so-similar situations. Then the person makes his decision.

As you can see, even a simple decision that will only affect one person involves a very complex process. Now think about decisions that are made as part of a team. As you can imagine, the complexity and the nature of the decision-making process in a team environment change because of group dynamics. In general, problem solving can lead to much better decisions when a team is utilized to call on its depth and breadth of experience. However, navigating a team through the proper steps of effectively involving every member and including the varying perspectives that may exist can be quite a challenge.

For teams that have a good working relationship and a moderate to high level of cohesiveness, the following method of problem solving and decision making is the best model.

THE REFLECTIVE-THINKING METHOD OF PROBLEM SOLVING

You have probably used the *reflective-thinking* method to solve problems in the past, but weren't even aware that you were using it. The *reflective-thinking* method of problem solving for groups is a straightforward approach to breaking down problem solving into five tasks.

1. Defining the problem

Sometimes, half the battle of solving a problem is clearly defining what the problem really is, and defining it in a clear and concise manner is always the best first step.

Team perspective:
Groups are typically better at defining the problem than individuals because they can bring more information to bear on the problem.

For the best results:

- Each member should take a turn describing her view of the particular problem or situation.

- No discussions: This step is not a discussion or a debate period, but one in which ideas are generated regarding the definition of the problem only.

- It is effective to have one member take the role of *scribe*, and write a summary of every member's definition on a white board where the whole team can see it.

- The member in the scribe role may have to moderate any questions that come up. Only questions that clarify the words or ideas can be asked.

- This step ends when each member has listed the problem in his own words and briefly described the problem from his point of view.

2. Analyzing the problem

During step two, the descriptions that were recorded in step one are open for discussion, and the team must reach a consensus on the qualities, characteristics, and definition of the problem.

Team perspective:

The more knowledge and different perspectives that can be included when determining what the real problem is and what the objectives of the decision-making process should be, the higher the quality of the decision. Teams are at their best when constructively analyzing problems.

For the best results:

- Members must focus only on the problem, not on the solutions.
- Clarify the extent of the problem.
- Discussion of the problem should include personal perspectives on and examples of the problem.
- Debate on different philosophies can take place.

- Important data should be analyzed: statistics and third-party examples could be utilized.

- The problem can be compared and contrasted to other similar problems.

- Draft a problem statement that clearly identifies what the problem is, who is affected by it, and what values are associated with it.

- End step two by also drafting a solution question, which asks how you will be solving the problem, and will help the team later in step four of the process.

Examples of Problem Statements and Solution Questions

Problem Statement	Solution Question
Ineffective:	*Ineffective:*
Our office isn't sure of our goals and we don't feel like we fit in with the rest of the company.	*How can our office have goals and fit in better within the company?*
Effective:	*Effective:*
Our office lacks an understanding of the company's mission and needs to adopt specific and clear goals that will shape our identity and build cohesion with each other and the rest of the company.	*What specific goals would best help our office reflect the mission of the company and positively reflect our unique identity? What items can we include in our goals that will help us build unity in our office and establish tighter bonds with headquarters and other offices?*

Practice A:

Think of a problem or opportunity that you have to consider at work. Using what you know of the *reflective-thinking* model of problem solving:

1. Define the problem or opportunity and write it down.

2. Draft both a problem statement and a solution question.

3. Establishing criteria for the solutions

In this step the team decides what conditions the solution will have to meet, or what elements it should include before trying to come up with solutions. For example, if your team is trying to pick a new logo for the business, you may list several criteria such as: 1) it shouldn't have a swoosh, 2) it has to look good in black and white and in a two-inch square space, and 3) it has to have our initials in it somewhere. The criteria chosen in this step will help the team evaluate potential solutions when it is time, and will save the team much time needlessly arguing about solutions that aren't optimal.

Team perspective:

More collective knowledge and varied perspectives enable a group to identify more criteria than an individual working on the same problem. However, if a leader doesn't facilitate this process, the team could get hung up debating criteria for too long.

For the best results:

- The criteria must be relevant to the problem at hand.

- The criteria must be discussed before coming up with the solution.

- In discussing the criteria the team should consider the following:

    — The strength of the solution: Does the criteria address the overall effectiveness of the solution? Does it account for all consequences?

    — Resources: Can the criteria be met given the specific resources that the team or company has to work with?

    — Ethics: Does the criteria test the solution for moral, ethical, or legal validity? Does it consider any ethical implications to employees, the environment, the community?

Practice B:

Using the problem or opportunity from earlier:

1. Write down criteria for your problem or opportunity choice.

4. Generating solutions

This step of problem solving involves generating as many relevant ideas as possible regarding a solution. Evaluating the different possibilities will take place in a later step, so this step should not be a discussion, but should be a brainstorming session, where members can throw out many good ideas and not have to worry about explaining or justifying them.

Team perspective:

Brainstorming works well in a group environment, where the diversity of ideas and inclusion of multiple perspectives leads to more creative thought processes. If each member's creativity is channeled effectively and the group's leadership maintains a unified focus while allowing for unique perspectives to be heard, groups can generate higher-quality solution alternatives than individuals.

For the best results:

- Appoint a member to serve as the scribe and to keep questions to a minimum and stop discussion.

- Begin with a reading of the problem statement and the solution question.

- No ideas for a solution are dismissed, no matter how bizarre or impossible they may initially sound. Some of the best ideas are at first seen as impossible or ridiculous.

- Each idea is written on a whiteboard or flip chart where the whole team can see it.

- At the end of this step, the scribe needs to read each idea out so that everyone has a chance to hear it. Duplicates should be consolidated.

5. Evaluating the solutions

In order to choose one of the solutions or to build the best solution, each of the ideas in step four is measured against the criteria from step three. Sometimes the solutions as they stand won't meet the criteria. The group can either merge ideas and build a better solution, or select the solution that covers the most criteria.

Team perspective:

Varied perspectives and a diversity of experience make groups superior to individuals when it comes to evaluating and judging alternative solutions. Group participation in the problem-solving steps of the *reflective-thinking* process leads to greater acceptance, commitment, and motivation among members; however, because of individual differences of opinion among members, teams can present a challenge in the selection step.

For the best results:

- A leader must take a strong role in facilitating this step, because it can be the hardest in which to reach agreement.

- The leader should read the problem statement and the solution question at the start of this step.

- The team should avoid compromises that will lessen the effectiveness of the solution.

CHAPTER SUMMARY

- Effective decision making involves several problem-solving and critical-thinking steps.

- The *reflective-thinking* method of problem solving works well for teams that are already formed, or where members are good communicators.

Skill Building

Ask a friend to help you generate possible solutions that fit your criteria for the problem or opportunity that you have been working on in the practice exercises earlier in this chapter.

CHAPTER | 19

ALTERNATIVE METHODS FOR PROBLEM SOLVING IN WORK GROUPS

LEARNING OBJECTIVES

After reading this chapter you should be able to:

- select an effective group problem-solving technique for any group situation
- participate effectively using the Nomitive Group Technique, the Delphi Technique, or any of the Advocate Techniques

ALTERNATE METHODS FOR GROUP PROBLEM SOLVING AND DECISION MAKING

While the *reflective-thinking* method of problem solving and decision making discussed in chapter 18 is quite effective for teams that work well together, it is not as effective for other types of work groups where members aren't as skilled in team communications or are geographically dispersed and can't physically meet. Often the issues may be so emotionally charged or personal that you don't want members meeting face to face.

Nominal Group Technique

The Nominal Group Technique, often referred to as NGT, is a method of problem solving and decision making that allows for a group of people to meet physically, but it doesn't allow for as much discussion among members as the *reflective-thinking* model. *NGT* minimizes interpersonal communications, hence the term *nominal* in the title. By cutting down on the interaction between group members, the problem-solving and decision-making process is much more efficient in cases where a team has just been formed and its members don't really know each other, or when a group is formed to deal with one specific problem or issue and will then disband.

The chief advantage of the *NGT* procedure is that everyone independently considers the problem or issue without influence from other group members. The challenging issues of communication and group dynamics don't really interfere with the process, yet the solution reflects a broad perspective and accounts for everyone's point of view. NGT uses a five-step approach.

1. Preparation
The group leader or facilitator defines the problem, issue, or challenge, drafts a solution question to present to the group, and plans the logistics of the meeting.

For the best results:
- Solution questions should be succinct and cover only one issue. (See the example in chapter 18.)

- The facilitator should have a flip chart and tape, so she can write ideas down on a sheet, tear it off, and tape it on the wall for everyone to see.

- The facilitator should prepare an opening presentation that explains the remaining four steps and highlights the relevance and importance of the solution to rest of the organization.

2. Silent generation of ideas

After the facilitator makes his introductory presentation and the group has been asked the solution question(s), the members are asked to silently think about and jot down their ideas regarding the question(s).

For the best results:

- The facilitator should allot a specific amount of time—no less than three minutes and no more than 10 minutes.
- Members should work silently and independently of each other.
- Members should be encouraged to write down phrases or brief sentences.

3. Round-Robin Recording

During this step, the facilitator will solicit one idea from each group member and write it down on the flip chart, making sure to tear off each page as it fills and hang it on the wall so the entire group can see the results. The facilitator will go through each member, then repeat the process until all the ideas are out on the board.

For the best results:

- No discussion, elaboration, or feedback is allowed during this step.
- No ideas that have already been posted are re-posted.
- Each idea is numbered, to make voting much easier.

4. Discussion

This step involves a brief discussion to clarify any potential confusion regarding the posted ideas. As the facilitator reads each idea, she asks the group if they have any questions or need any clarification.

For the best results:

- Allow for any member to clarify any idea, not just the ones he personally provided.

- No expression of opinions, personal commentary, or debate is allowed.

- No voting takes place during this step.

5. Voting

This is the final step, when group members can make a decision about the ideas that have been posted. Voting is done on index cards, in order to keep this process anonymous and to keep peer pressure from affecting members' votes. Usually a clear-winning idea emerges. If a tie does occur, then members have to vote again, but only the ideas that tied are included in the vote.

For the best results:

- Each member gets five index cards.

- Each member writes what he considers the five best ideas, one on each card.

- The members then rank their five best ideas by putting a rank number in a circle in the top left corner of the index card. (A five represents the highest score and accompanies their vote for the best idea, and a four for the next best pick, etc.)

- The leader collects the cards when everyone is finished and tallies findings at the front of the room where everyone can see the scores.

Practice A:

Think of a situation where NGT would be more effective than the *reflective-thinking* method of problem solving for teams. Write it down.

Possible Answer:

If the group is new or is temporary (they exist for the purpose of this decision only), then NGT would be perfect. In cases where traditional methods of group dialogue, or the *reflective-thinking* technique has resulted in less than optimum decisions or has caused too much friction, NGT could be more effective.

The Delphi Technique

In contrast to *NGT*, the Delphi technique allows for a group decision to be made with the decision participants never actually meeting or discussing the problem, concern, or issue. Instead, a problem is identified, and members are guided through a series of carefully designed questionnaires to provide potential solutions. By removing all chances of interference from group dynamics, the *Delphi* technique can be quite effective when you need to get the perspectives of varied viewpoints, and the members either can't physically be together, or the topic is controversial and the members wish to keep their views anonymous.

The Delphi technique works best if the decision participants are experts in the field that the problem, concern, or issue is in. Usually questionnaires are distributed, either by mail or electronically to the group. Each member completes the questionnaire independently of one another and sends in his response. Responses are tabulated from the original questionnaire and a new questionnaire is devised which uses the data collected in the first Delphi round to focus in on a specific area of the problem or potential solution to the problem. The questionnaires continue until the group's opinions begin to show a consensus on a prospective solution to the problem.

The Delphi technique includes three steps:

1. Selecting a response group

- The response group should be made up of only experts in the subject matter, topic, or field of inquiry.

- It is important to reinforce the fact that each member's identity will remain anonymous.

- A copy of the results is promised to each member.

2. Administering the questionnaires

- The original set of questions should begin to narrow the inquiry and can be more general than later rounds. For example, original questions may be open-ended and ask for an answer to a question as general as 'What issues regarding [the topic] are important to you?'

- Second and third round questionnaires should reflect the first-round questions and provide a sense of consistency for the members. For example, if the first questionnaire utilized the question in the example above, then the second round might list five of the most frequent responses and ask members to rank their interest in these areas. Then each member gets a sense of where her opinion falls in comparison to the groups norms. This will facilitate more openness and cooperation from the participants.

- True-false questions and closed-ended questions tend to increase the effectiveness of questionnaires in later rounds.

3. Analyzing and evaluating results

- Data should be analyzed, evaluated, and applied to further question-naires until a solution emerges or can be inferred from the data.

- A *results* document or presentation should be developed as accurately and expeditiously as possible.

Practice B:

Think of an example where the Delphi technique would be the best way to make an effective decision in a group environment.

Possible Answer:

The ABC Marketing Company has been growing fast. Executives attribute the success to the 12 regional sales managers. The managers will be attending a weeklong seminar in Hawaii. The executives of the company plan to take advantage of this situation (having all their stars in one place at one time) to find out about some of the key issues that make their managers so effective. However, they also want to find out about how their managers feel on two very personal and possibly emotional/confrontational issues. Should the company allow benefits for gay managers' same-sex partners? Should the company institute a random drug testing policy for management?

Since these questions can be considered volatile, the executives could use the Delphi technique over the course of the week, with managers receiving and handing in new questionnaires each day, based on the previous day's findings.

Advocacy Techniques

In some instances the leader of the group or team may decide to use an *advocacy technique* in order to guarantee that the group identifies and analyzes several alternative positions. By forcing members to look at alternative positions, members are forced to consider strengths and weaknesses, advantages and disadvantages of multiple viewpoints.

If a group has been together for a long time and members tend to always agree with one another, or the issues surrounding the problem or concern are very controversial, an advocacy technique may be helpful for effective problem solving.

Devil's Advocate Technique

For groups that exhibit groupthink—where members tend to agree with each on everything and decisions are often weak due to a lack of opposing or varied viewpoints—appointing a *devil's advocate* can be the most effective way to introduce alternative viewpoints to the group in the decision-making process.

The assigned devil's advocate is charged with raising challenges to the group's ideas and recommendations and introducing dissent into the decision-making process.

Tips for assigning a devil's advocate:

- Choose a member who is both competent and credible—they must be taken seriously by the other members of the group.

- Select a particular step of the problem-solving process to engage in, such as when analyzing the problem or when establishing the criteria for the solution.

- Make sure they are coached in critical-thinking skills and effective argumentative techniques.

Multiple Advocacy

This approach is similar to the devil's advocate approach, in that individual members are assigned a position or a stance regarding the decision to be made. Unlike the former approach, however, where one member represents opposing views, there are several members who all represent different, opposing views. Usually individuals are assigned a position that reflects the ideas of a specific subgroup of the organization.

For example, if the team has been assembled to discuss changing the cafeteria menu, then it would be effective to assign several members to take the position of particular subgroups. Jorge would be responsible for representing the Spanish and Latino opinions; while Allison would represent the night crew; and Jon the organic eaters of the company.

When utilizing the *multiple advocacy* technique, each team member involved in the decision process must carry out the appropriate positions in all subsequent dialogue, discussion, and/or voting.

Dialectical Inquiry

This technique is similar to the devil's advocate approach in that the advocate opposes the majority. However, in the *dialectical inquiry* method, the advocate is assigned the role of questioning the underlying assumptions associated with the identification of the problem and the solution criteria. The advocate has as his mission the undermining and/or exposing of the assumptions underlying the plan.

The job of the advocate begins by identifying the prevailing view of the problem and its associated assumptions. The member then develops an alternative problem that is credible and rests on different assumptions. In doing so, the accuracy of and the ability to generalize the original assumption is examined and possibly altered. As a result, group members are forced to look at new ways to analyze and solve the problem.

CHAPTER SUMMARY

- Many models and techniques exist for making effective group decisions.

- The Nominal Group Technique works best for groups that aren't good at communicating with each other. The Delphi Technique works effectively for groups that can't or shouldn't meet face to face. Advocacy Techniques exist for groups that have been around so long that they exhibit groupthink, and for team members who represent a constituency.

Skill Building

Have you ever been involved in a team that utilized any of the alternative group decision-making strategies in this chapter?

If yes:

- Did the method you used enable your group to make the most effective decision? Explain.
- Would another method have worked as well or better? Explain.
- How did your experience compare to the models described here? Explain.

For the future:

- The next time you are involved in a situation where one of these methods would work to help your team or group make an effective decision, try to play the appropriate lead role, scribe, or advocate and notice how the group reacts to your lead.

CHAPTER | 20

EVALUATING AND IMPROVING TEAM PERFORMANCE

LEARNING OBJECTIVES

After reading this chapter you should be able to:

- monitor team and individual performance
- use observations and feedback to improve team performance
- conduct a Formal Performance Evaluation

IMPROVING TEAM PERFORMANCE

The ultimate criteria for evaluating team performance is whether or not the team meets the task goals it set out to accomplish. Answering the following two basic questions will tell you whether the team performed successfully or not:

1. Did the team accomplish its overall mission?

2. Did the team meet its specific task goals on a timely basis?

However, merely evaluating whether the team reaches its goals or not will not help develop a better team or better team members.

The goal of evaluating team performance should be to improve team performance.

The most effective way to improve team performance through evaluation is to provide two levels of performance evaluations:

Level 1. Observations and Behavioral Feedback
Level 2. Formal Performance Evaluations

OBSERVATIONS AND BEHAVIORAL FEEDBACK

The most effective method of managing team performance through evaluations is the routine task of observing individual and team work habits and providing constructive feedback about those habits as they are observed. Feedback should always be based on observable actions, attitudes, behaviors, statements, and results. Constructive feedback should be used to guide the social and emotional growth of team members and to provide the team with a continuous indicator as to the state of the team's cohesion and productivity.

Team leaders, managers, and team members should all be focused on routinely observing the performance of the team's members, and offering constructive feedback to reinforce good behavior and to improve questionable behavior.

When team members use observations to give behavioral feedback, they should follow the methods for giving constructive feedback as described in chapter 16 and the tips for resolving conflict in chapter 17. Follow these additional guidelines for giving behavioral feedback, especially if you are the team leader or manager:

1. Make sure your feedback is accurate, timely, and positive.

- Describe only observed behavior: what you saw or thought you saw, not what you think the other person meant or thought.

- Be specific about the time, the place, the conditions, etc.

- Make sure any supporting data is verifiable.

- Deliver the feedback as soon as possible.

- If you are delivering corrective feedback you can still be positive in your approach by mentioning a positive observation first.

Example:

Gywn: "Jon, I would consider you one of the most professional and effective reps in our division of the company. Yet, I noticed in the service-team meeting earlier today that you did not have any notes nor did you participate in the discussion of the Newberg project. Furthermore, Rich informed me that you were scheduled to attend the seminar on 'Effective Customer Service Negotiating Techniques' last Friday, the 24th and you didn't show and didn't notify anyone."

2. Before you interpret the behavior, you should invite the other party to give you any additional information or explanations.

It is always good practice, particularly if you are a manager or team leader, to give the recipient of your feedback a chance to respond to you before you deliver your interpretation. You may find out something that you didn't know or that changes your interpretation of the behavior and, therefore, your message.

Example:

Gwyn: "Jon, you have never had any attendance or performance problems in the past, so why don't you tell me what is going on with you right now?"

Jon: "Well Gywn, last Tuesday my wife was referred to a cancer specialist because her doctor was alarmed at the results of her latest tests. I was able to pull some strings and I got her into the Cancer Research Center for a full battery of tests. The only day available was last Friday, and quite frankly, I thought that being with her was more important than attending the seminar. I guess I just didn't want everyone at the office talking about 'poor Jon's wife' so I kind of kept it to myself. I figured that my record and my performance has been excellent and one missed seminar shouldn't hurt my effectiveness or that of the team's. As far as today's meeting, my head is just not here. We should be getting the results back from the cancer center at any time today, and I just can't think of anything else right now."

3. Tie the behavior that you have described to the impact or consequences that it had/has on the team and/or the team's performance.

- After getting clarification of how the individual sees his own behavior you can then adjust your feedback to have maximum impact.

- Tying behavior to the impact it has on performance, especially if it affects other team members, will substantiate the feedback for the individual. This gives him an emotional reason to listen to the feedback and to adjust his behavior accordingly.

Example:

Gwyn: "Wow, Jon, I didn't know anything was wrong. I had no idea what you and your wife have been going through. If there is anything that I can do to help please let me know. As far as the seminar and the meeting goes, don't worry about it, I completely understand and so will your colleagues. As far as keeping things secret about your wife, that's fine. I would, however, like to tell your team that you need to be with your family for an emergency and that is why you missed the seminar last week and will be going home early today. They deserve to know something and I don't think it is fair to leave them totally in the dark. Please take the rest of the day off to be with your wife and call me the minute you hear anything."

Practice:

You catch your teammate making up numbers for his weekly sales report. You believe that he is *padding the books*—putting appointments down that he didn't attend—because: a) you have a friend at the office your teammate supposedly visited last week and she has told you that no one at her office has visited with your teammate, and b) you saw your teammate in the bar around the corner when he was supposed to be on an appointment uptown.

You don't want to be a snitch, so you think the best approach is to deal with the problem without going to management. How do you effectively give your teammate feedback so he understands that his actions are wrong, and that they may be impacting the rest of the team?

Possible Answer:

You may wish to enlist another team member to help you, so that you can give the feedback in a more formal or public setting. You also might have more impact if the feedback session includes another teammate. You would start by telling your teammate that you are concerned for him and for the team because of his behavior. You state what you think you saw, using as much detail as possible, including dates and the name of the company you know he didn't visit. Then you give him a chance to explain. If he has an explanation that suffices then you act accordingly, but if his explanation is merely a flimsy excuse or a lie to avoid further action, then you must relay to him that his behavior is hurting the group. You can tell him that if he continues to hurt the team, you have a responsibility to take further action, because you have the right as a team member to take such action, but that you wish he would correct his behavior before such a step is necessary.

FORMAL PERFORMANCE EVALUATIONS

While observations and behavioral feedback should be a part of the everyday work environment of every team, *formal performance evaluations (FPEs)* are certainly not a part of the everyday work environment of every team. FPEs are important elements of the company's overall management strategy that are specifically designed to assess and develop the individual performance of every employee. Depending on the size and scope of the evaluation, they can be scheduled yearly, quarterly, or monthly, and are usually held yearly.

Formal performance evaluations are the subject of much consideration in management circles today. Articles in journals, entire books, and even graduate level management courses are devoted to the subject of performance appraisals. This chapter will not attempt to summarize the theory behind *performance management*; rather, it will outline the main components of an effective formal performance evaluation for a team environment.

A formal performance evaluation used in a team environment can be very helpful in analyzing and improving team performance. It should focus on the both the team's success and that of every individual member. The team leader or manager conducts the evaluation with each member separately, covering both team performance issues as well as individual performance issues.

The FPE encompasses several meetings (at least two) for each team member in which the team leader or manager reviews past performance evaluations, summarizes current behavior and performance ratings, and makes recommendations for performance improvements.

It is important that the ratings methods that are used in the formal performance evaluation are standardized and known by the employees ahead of time. The ratings methodology must be standardized in order to provide significance to the team as a whole. It wouldn't make sense to measure employees up against different yardsticks, and it would be ineffective as a tool for improving their behavior and/or skills. Some leaders prefer to have members use the rating system to evaluate their own performance and the performance of each team member as well.

On the next page is an example of an evaluation form that can be used to give team members a rating for their performance evaluation. As you will notice, the evaluation form should cover both task and behavioral accomplishments.

CHAPTER SUMMARY

- In order to improve the performance on a team, managers or team leaders observe members' behavior and give them constant feedback on how to improve themselves.

- Managers and team leaders can also use formal evaluations to improve team performance.

Skill Building

Use the evaluation form at the end of this chapter and fill it out for yourself first. Then fill it out for other members of your work team.

How do you rate yourself compared to others in your team?

After rating yourself, do you see any areas where you need improvement?

Where are you strongest?

If you fill out the evaluation for other members in your team, can you look at the total score and see what areas of team skills your team needs the most work in?

Formal Performance Evaluation for Team Member:

Rank the usual behavior, attitude, or performance displayed by the above team member in each of the categories described below:

GOALS & LEADERSHIP
Member participates in team goal setting:

1	2	3	4	5	6	7	8	9	10

Rarely involved in team goal-setting process.

Sometimes offers input to help the team define goals.

Often participates in the development of team goals and works with others to clarify meaning.

Member's behavior is consistent with team goals:

1	2	3	4	5	6	7	8	9	10

Often chooses to work on tasks linked to personal goals, not team goals.

Works towards team goals when not in competition with personal goals.

Often chooses team tasks over those associated with personal goals.

Member shares leadership roles:

1	2	3	4	5	6	7	8	9	10

Often dominates discussions regardless of skills and abilities and directs team-subverting behavior.

Often competes with others for visibility; sometimes exerts influence to encourage team-subverting behavior.

Actively takes leadership role when his or her own skills and abilities can be used to further the team's goals.

TASK ROLES
Member proposes new ideas to accomplish tasks:

1	2	3	4	5	6	7	8	9	10

Often resists new ideas; criticizes new plans; finds a way to "stop progress in its tracks."

Often organizes other member's ideas into coherent solution; clarifies task assignments.

Frequently initiates problem-solving process and offers ideas to "get things done."

Member works with others to accomplish tasks:

1	2	3	4	5	6	7	8	9	10

Rarely does the required work; actively stalls to cover up for being unprepared.

Usually puts the required effort into the task to help get the job done; sometimes needs encouragement.

Actively sets an example for others by jumping right in, even if skills are lacking in particular area.

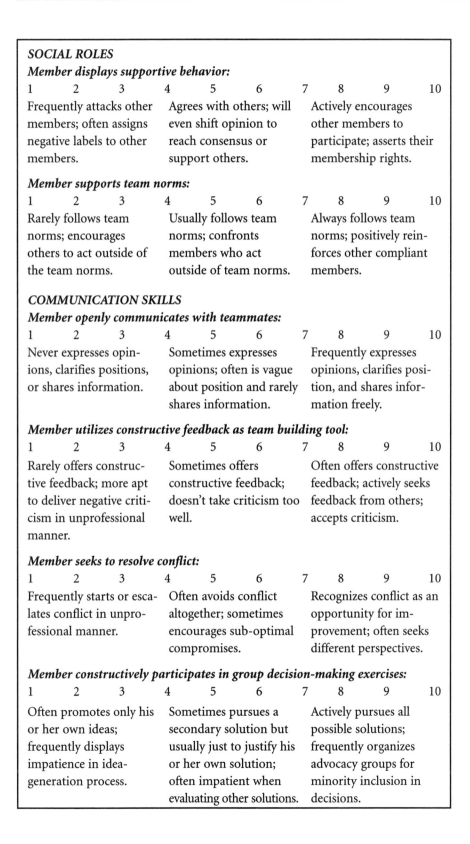

SOCIAL ROLES
Member displays supportive behavior:

| 1 | 2 | 3 | 4 | 5 | 6 | 7 | 8 | 9 | 10 |

Frequently attacks other members; often assigns negative labels to other members.

Agrees with others; will even shift opinion to reach consensus or support others.

Actively encourages other members to participate; asserts their membership rights.

Member supports team norms:

| 1 | 2 | 3 | 4 | 5 | 6 | 7 | 8 | 9 | 10 |

Rarely follows team norms; encourages others to act outside of the team norms.

Usually follows team norms; confronts members who act outside of team norms.

Always follows team norms; positively reinforces other compliant members.

COMMUNICATION SKILLS
Member openly communicates with teammates:

| 1 | 2 | 3 | 4 | 5 | 6 | 7 | 8 | 9 | 10 |

Never expresses opinions, clarifies positions, or shares information.

Sometimes expresses opinions; often is vague about position and rarely shares information.

Frequently expresses opinions, clarifies position, and shares information freely.

Member utilizes constructive feedback as team building tool:

| 1 | 2 | 3 | 4 | 5 | 6 | 7 | 8 | 9 | 10 |

Rarely offers constructive feedback; more apt to deliver negative criticism in unprofessional manner.

Sometimes offers constructive feedback; doesn't take criticism too well.

Often offers constructive feedback; actively seeks feedback from others; accepts criticism.

Member seeks to resolve conflict:

| 1 | 2 | 3 | 4 | 5 | 6 | 7 | 8 | 9 | 10 |

Frequently starts or escalates conflict in unprofessional manner.

Often avoids conflict altogether; sometimes encourages sub-optimal compromises.

Recognizes conflict as an opportunity for improvement; often seeks different perspectives.

Member constructively participates in group decision-making exercises:

| 1 | 2 | 3 | 4 | 5 | 6 | 7 | 8 | 9 | 10 |

Often promotes only his or her own ideas; frequently displays impatience in idea-generation process.

Sometimes pursues a secondary solution but usually just to justify his or her own solution; often impatient when evaluating other solutions.

Actively pursues all possible solutions; frequently organizes advocacy groups for minority inclusion in decisions.

APPENDIX

ADDITIONAL RESOURCES

Teamwork

Eicholz, Marti, et al. *Business Relationships: The Dynamics of Teamwork.* 1997.

Gartner, Robert. *High Performance Through Teamwork.* 1996.

MacKall, Dandi Daley. *Teamwork Skills (The Career Skills Library).* 1997.

Pucel, David J., and Rosemary T. Fruehling. *Working in Teams: Interaction and Communication.* 1997.

Syer, John, and Christopher Connolly (Contributor). *How Teamwork Works: The Dynamics of Effective Team Development.* 1996.

Wilson, Jack, and Inc. Associates. *Effective Teamwork.* 1995.

Business Communications

Adelstein, Michael E., and W. Keats Sparrow. *Business Communications.* 1990.

Barfield, Ray E., et al. *Business Communications (Barron's Business Library)*. 1992.

Been, Marta. *Say It Right, Write It Right: The Secretary's Guide to Solving Business Communications Problems*. 1994.

Cullinan, Mary P. *Business Communications Principles and Processes*. 1997.

De Bonis, J. Nicholas (Contributor), et al. *AMA Handbook for Managing Business to Business Marketing Communications*. 1997.

Flower, Linda, and John Ackerman. *Writers at Work: Strategies for Communications in Business and Professional Settings*. 1997.

Galle, William P., and Maurice F. Villere. *Business Communications*. 1996.

Hemphill, Phyllis Davis, and Donald W. McCormick. *Business Communications with Writing Improvement Exercises*. 1991.

Himstreet, William C. *Business Communications: A Guide to Effective Writing, Speaking and Listening*. 1982.

Lehman, Carol M., and Deborah Daniel Dufrene. *Business Communications*. 1998.

McManus, Judith A. *Effective Business Speaking: The Basics Made Easy*. LearningExpress, 1998.

Moreno, Mary. *The Writer's Guide to Corporate Communications*. 1997.

Murphy, Herta A., and Herbert W. Hildebrandt. (Contributor). *Effective Business Communications*. 1996.

Ober, Scot. *Contemporary Business Communications*. 1998.

Miscellaneous

Prentice Hall's Get a Grip on Speaking and Listening: Vital Communication Skills for Today's Business World Corporate Classrooms. Prentice Hall, 1995.

Brownell, Judi. *Building Active Listening Skills*. Prentice Hall, 1986.

———. *Listening: Attitudes, Principles, and Skill*. Prentice Hall, 1995.

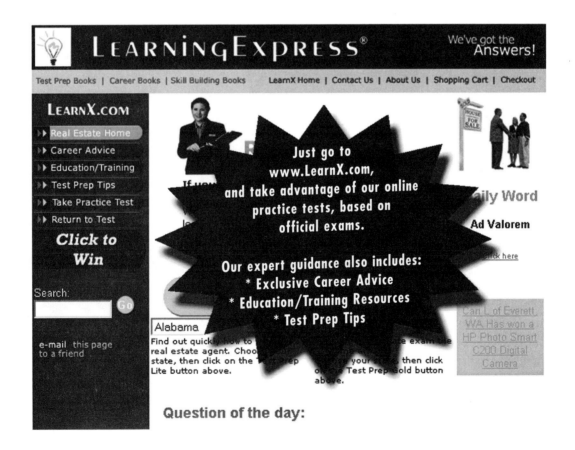